# Contents

# Murderesses in Victorian Britain

## By

## Christina Croft

# Chapter 1 – Hanged By The Neck

On a drizzly Saturday morning in August 1856, a sixteen-year-old apprentice architect made his way to Dorchester Gaol in anticipation of the day's entertainment. Despite the inclement weather, a crowd of over three thousand people had gathered in front of the stage to await the appearance of the star of the show: forty-five-year-old Elizabeth *Martha* Brown. Her co-star, the bushy-bearded William Calcraft, was already enjoying the audience's attention as he moved across the stage, armed with a selection of ropes and a white hood.

The spectators might have presumed that, with over a quarter of a century's experience, fifty-five-year-old Calcraft would have mastered the art of a paid executioner. Unfortunately for his victims, though, he favoured 'the short drop' of only three feet, which meant that, rather than dying instantly, prisoners were often left squirming for several minutes in the agonies of a slow strangulation. Their only hope was that their friends would rush forwards to pull their legs to hasten their demise – a service which Calcraft himself sometimes performed with great theatricality, even going so far as to climb onto the shoulders of one writhing prisoner.

At length, a hush descended on the crowd as Martha, dressed in black silk, emerged through the prison doors and calmly ascended the first few steps of the stage. Calcraft swiftly and silently bound her hands before leading her up a further flight to the platform where he pulled the white hood over her head and fastened a rope around her legs to prevent her dress from rising up as she fell.

The rain was falling more steadily now, soaking the hood until it clung to Martha's features like a macabre death mask. Calcraft placed the noose around her neck; a sudden clack of a bolt echoed on the prison walls, followed by a sickening thud as she fell through the trap door and began the horrific process of asphyxiation.

In return for his services, the hangman received one guinea[a] to supplement his five-pounds a quarter retainer. More lucratively, though, he was allowed to keep whatever possessions a prisoner brought to the scaffold, and these could be sold to travelling fares to be viewed by curiosity-seekers in much the same way as pious pilgrims viewed the relics of a saint. Alternatively, the clothes could be sold to Madame Tussaud's to add a gruesome authenticity to the waxworks in the Chamber of Horrors.

> "As profitable," wrote one of Calcraft's contemporaries, "have proved the sale of the various ropes which strangled the criminals, the hangman's tariff of prices rising from 5s. to £1 per inch, according to the notoriety of a criminal, the circumstances of purchasers, and the pressure of demand for a piece of the curiosity."[1]

Having been left hanging for an hour, Martha's body was cut down and placed in a coffin at the foot of the scaffold; and, when the medical officer had confirmed that she was dead, a death mask was taken of her face before she was buried in an unmarked grave within the confines of the prison. Calcraft returned home with his spoils, and the whole sorry episode might have been forgotten were it not for the presence of the apprentice architect: a young Thomas Hardy.

Although this was not the first execution that he had witnessed, Hardy was haunted by the memory of 'how the tight black silk gown set off her shape as she wheeled half-round and back.' The image made so deep an impression upon him that, years later, he would immortalise Martha's demise in his novel *Tess of the D'Urbevilles*.

In some ways Martha's story was as tragic as that of Hardy's eponymous heroine, for she, too, struggled to be

[a] 21 shillings or £1.1.0 – the equivalent to £1.05 post-decimalisation.

free from a humdrum existence only to be disappointed by those whom she hoped would save her. Like Tess, Martha, the daughter of dairyman, began her working life as a milkmaid, but, at the age of twenty in 1831, she saw an opportunity to escape from her exhausting duties by marrying Bernard Bearn, a widowed butcher who was looking for a wife to raise his two motherless children.

Although nineteen years younger than her husband, Martha was happy for the first five years of her marriage. Initial tensions between herself and her nine-year-old stepdaughter gradually eased; and, from the start, she and her seven-year-old stepson were devoted to one another. The birth of two boys of her own added to her joy, but the domestic bliss was short-lived as her elder son died of typhoid before his third birthday, and his younger brother died of the same disease a couple of weeks later. Soon afterwards, her stepson was killed in an accident and, a decade after the wedding, Bernard also died.

Unlike many widows of the era, Martha was not left destitute, as Bernard had bequeathed her fifty pounds[b]. Moreover, she soon found work as a housekeeper at Blackmanston Farm in the Dorset countryside, the home of two unmarried brothers with whom she remained for over ten years.

In the course of her work, she made the acquaintance of a handsome young shepherd, John Brown, who, despite being almost half her age, eventually proposed. Whether he was drawn to her pretty face or her fifty pounds savings is open to conjecture but Martha, flattered by his attention, accepted his offer and the couple were soon married. Leaving Blackmanston Farm, they settled in the nearby village of Birdsmoregate, where Martha ran a grocer's shop, and John set himself up as a pedlar.

---

[b] Approximately £7,000 in today's values.

Unfortunately, Martha soon discovered that, as her husband moved from town to town selling his wares, he was travelling as much for pleasure as for business. The more he drank and philandered, the greater became the tension in the household, which often erupted into heated arguments during which John beat and punched her.

John's brutal treatment of Martha would not have been viewed as exceptional, as, under the law, a man had the right to expect total obedience from his wife, who was merely his appendage or chattel. Just as a slave took the name of his master, a married woman took her husband's name to signify that she was his property, and he was free to use his property in any way that he chose. He was well within his rights to beat her, providing he applied the 'rule of thumb' and did not strike her with anything broader than that digit.

By the mid-nineteenth century, attitudes were beginning to change as more enlightened politicians called for greater protection for wives. Lord Palmerston argued that a woman was entitled to expect a husband to protect her; and his fellow M.P., Thomas Finn, pointed out that a man could be brought to court for stealing dead wood or crops, and women deserved at least the same rights as twigs and vegetables.

> "One's mind actually recoiled," Henry Fitzroy told the House of Commons, "when he thought of the dastardly and cowardly assaults which were being constantly perpetrated upon defenceless women by brutes who called themselves men."[2]

In 1853, the Act for the Better Prevention and Punishment of Aggravated Assaults upon Women and Children went some way to protecting wives from violent husbands, but the majority of domestic abuse cases remained unreported and thousands of women like Martha Brown were trapped in loveless and abusive marriages. Many lived in fear of their husbands, particularly when they had been drinking – a problem so extensive that one sympathetic coroner reported:

"It is not at all unusual to hear of a case in which a husband…has come home intoxicated, and has been left to die on the floor of a room, or even of a passage, because the finder has feared the outburst of bad temper which so often follows when one sleeping off a drunken bout is disturbed. Such deaths are generally due to coma from apoplexy and cerebral congestion."[3]

Matters came to a head for Martha Brown on the night of 5th July 1856, when John returned home late from the tavern and she accused him of having been gallivanting with one of their neighbours. He responded by striking her with a heavy horsewhip and, when she screamed, he kicked her roughly, telling her that he hoped that she would be dead by the morning. Incensed, dazed and fearing for her life, she reached for the nearest object: an axe that she had been using to stoke the fire. With all the strength she could muster, she brought the blade down on his head, sending him reeling to the floor. All the months of repressed anger at the abuse and humiliation to which he had subjected her, suddenly exploded and she struck him again and again although he lay unmoving.

Coincidentally, five years earlier, another John Brown had met an equally violent end at the hands of his wife, Jane, in almost identical circumstances. Like Martha's husband, the earlier John Brown was a hardened drinker, who regularly beat his wife until one fateful evening in 1851 when he pulled out a knife, and, in self-defence, she struck him a fatal blow with a poker. Witnesses attested to his drunkenness and 'bad character' and, consequently, Jane was sentenced to only six months imprisonment.

With sufficient calm and foresight, Martha, could also have claimed that she had acted in self-defence but, instead, she made the tragic mistake of lying about what had happened. For two hours she waited before running to a neighbour's house and screaming that John had been involved in a terrible accident. He had, she said, been kicked by a horse and had collapsed outside the cottage. She had managed to drag him indoors, where, for the past two hours he had clung to her so tightly that she had been unable to leave him until he died in her arms.

The neighbour summoned a policeman from the recently-formed Dorset County Constabulary, and, as soon as he arrived at the cottage, he realised that the story made no sense. Although John must have been bleeding heavily, there was no trail of blood leading indoors; and the wounds on John's head and face were entirely inconsistent with a kick from a horse.

In the case of a suspicious, sudden or unexplained death, the law required an inquest to be held under the auspices of a senior lawyer who had been appointed as the regional coroner. Being public events, inquests were held in the largest available room, which, in most cases, was in a tavern. A jury, comprising any number of local people, was presented with evidence and asked to decide whether death was due to natural causes, an accident, suicide or murder. If the conclusion was murder, any named suspect would be held in custody pending a trial at the next assizes[c].

The jury at John Brown's inquest was left in no doubt about the cause of death when the surgeon, who had performed a post-mortem, presented his evidence.

"The bones of the nose were broken;" he said, "there was a triangular wound exposing the bone above the left eyebrow, another triangular wound exposing the bone at the top of the head, and a third wound at the back of the head. The left ear was perforated; and behind it was a long wound divided

---

[c] Until 1971, assizes were courts held at regular intervals – usually quarterly – in each English and Welsh county.

into two. The frontal bone was fractured from the orbit, through the parietal into the occipital bone. Seven pieces of bone, varying in size from half an inch to three inches, had been driven into the brain, and a large quantity of blood was effused...The injuries were not such as a kick from a horse would explain; and...a man thus injured could not have held the prisoner by the clothes for two hours, so as to prevent her from seeking earlier for assistance. The facts showed that deceased had been killed by blows where the body was found."[4]

The jury had no option but to conclude that Martha had murdered her husband, and, a fortnight later, she stood in the dock at the Dorchester Assizes. The trial lasted for only one day and, when the jury returned a guilty verdict, the judge donned his black cap, signifying that he would pass the death sentence, and uttered the words that brought terror to the heart of every defendant:

"Elizabeth Martha Brown, you will be taken hence to the prison in which you were last confined and from there to a place of execution where you will be hanged by the neck until you are dead and thereafter your body buried within the precincts of the prison and may the Lord have mercy upon your soul."

On returning to the prison, Martha, like all convicts under a capital sentence, was placed in the larger execution cell, where she was watched night and day to prevent her from taking her own life before justice was enacted.

Customarily, there was a three-week interval between the passing of the sentence and the execution to allow for the presentation of petitions for a reprieve. Until 1837, such petitions were submitted directly to the monarch but, when Queen Victoria ascended the throne, it was felt that an eighteen-year-old girl should not be asked to make such momentous decisions, and, therefore, it was decided that henceforth they should be sent to the Home Secretary, who would act on behalf of the Crown.

Sadly, for Martha no reprieve was forthcoming, and, in the early hours of the morning of 7th August, she heard the hammering of the carpenters erecting the gallows.

"The scaffold," wrote the journalist, Henry Mayhew, "is about the size of a large caravan, the sides being let down, and a beam erected over it. The floor is composed of two parts, constructed so as to fall down to each side. The executioner touches a handle similar to a common pump handle, which detaches the bolt underneath, and the murderer is suspended by the neck in presence of the vast confluence of people."[5]

As was the custom, Martha was hanged in public in the hope that the spectacle would serve as a deterrent to other criminals; and as proof to the law-abiding citizens that justice had been served. Many influential people, however, were deeply disturbed that such sombre occasions had become a source of entertainment, drawing rowdy crowds from many miles around. Members of Parliament complained about obscene language and drunken behaviour, while the author, Charles Dickens, lamented the lack of decorum and the 'ribaldry, debauchery, levity, drunkenness, and flaunting vice in fifty other shapes.'[d]

In 1864, as opposition to public executions intensified, a Royal Commission was established to examine the merits and disadvantages of the practice. Two years later, the Commission's report was published and debated in Parliament, exciting strong opinions on both sides. The Conservative Peer, Lord Dunsany, argued that hangings carried out in private would be 'far more solemn and decorous than they [are] at present';[6] while the Foreign Secretary, Lord Malmesbury, reported that one of his servants was so shocked after witnessing such a macabre

---

[d] See Chapter 18

spectacle that he had been unable to work for several days afterwards. Others, like Lord St Leonards, continued to insist that the public had the right to see that justice was done, and the horror of witnessing a hanging was sufficient to turn even the most hardened criminal from his errant ways.

Ultimately, Lord Dunsany's argument won the day, and, in 1868, the Capital Punishment Amendment Act decreed that all future hangings would be carried out within the confines of the prison. As a concession to those who felt that the public should be involved the procedure, reporters were permitted to witness the event; and the tolling of a bell and the hoisting of a black flag above the prison would show the crowds outside that the sentence had been carried out.

Further discussions ensued about the suitability of the hangmen, some of whom were so notorious for their ineptitude that, rather than being seen as public servants, they were treated as pariahs. One Member of Parliament complained that, due to the hangmen's incompetence, 'a man was sometimes hanging fifteen or twenty minutes before life was entirely extinct'[7].

While William Calcraft appeared unruffled by such criticism, others were wounded by a lack of respect for their office.

> 'My position is not a pleasant one,' remarked William Marwood[e]; and James Berry recorded that, 'Personally I had a great distaste for the work, though I did not consider it in any way dishonourable or degrading.'[8]

Surprisingly, though, there was no shortage of applicants for the role, the majority of whom were motivated not only by the prospect of remuneration but also

---

[e] Marwood was the first hangman to introduce the 'long drop' by which a prisoner's neck was instantly broken, thus avoiding the unnecessary suffering of strangulation.

by a sense of moral duty. When, for example, James Berry was appointed to replace the notoriously inept and drunken Benjamin Binns, he was told that over a thousand other candidates had applied for the same position.

# Chapter 2 – The State is Justified

At the beginning of the nineteenth century, there were over two hundred capital crimes, ranging from treason and murder to staying with gypsies, impersonating a Chelsea Pensioner or even defacing Westminster Bridge. By the time that Queen Victoria ascended the throne in 1837, that number had been reduced through a series of Acts of Parliament and, over the next two decades, further reforms were introduced until, by 1861, only high treason, murder, piracy, and arson in a royal dockyard merited an appointment with the hangman.

Already, though, there were calls for a complete end to capital punishment as abolitionists argued that the number of hangings per year proved that it failed to serve as a deterrent. Moreover, they said, as judges and juries were not infallible, there was always the danger of hanging an innocent person. Many juries were so afraid of condemning the innocent to death that they returned a not guilty verdict, regardless of the evidence to the contrary; and a reporter for *The London Gazette* discovered cases where evidence had been deliberately suppressed for fear that it would lead to an execution:

> "Such conduct is disgraceful and is totally subversive of the administration of all justice. It strikes at the very safety of society; for it tends to shelter those who have been guilty of crimes affecting life; and the proof of which must in many instances rest almost entirely upon scientific evidence. We shall take care to expose any case of this kind that may come before us. An unintentional mistake or omission in medical evidence is pardonable; but the wilful suppression of facts and opinions, because they might, if expressed, lead to the capital conviction of a person charged with crime, admits neither of palliation nor excuse."[9]

For the most part, though, even the most ardent penal reformers believed that abolishing the death penalty would increase the number of murders. Without the threat of execution, burglars would be more inclined to kill their victims; and prisoners serving life sentences would have nothing to lose if they murdered their gaolers. Pious Victorian patriarchs cited Old Testament examples to 'prove' that God was in favour of capital punishment.

> "As a murderer," they claimed, "cannot with safety be allowed to work out his punishment and go free, there is no chance of his social reformation, and the State is justified in ridding itself of a pest."[10]

The abolitionists' cause was further undermined by graphic reports of violent murders, which prompted an outraged public to demand the severest sentence. The greatest indignation was reserved for women who committed mariticide[f], which undermined the idealised image of dutiful and subservient wives whose sole purpose was to please and obey their husbands. If women could kill their husbands without fear of being hanged, society would collapse and, as one judge pointed out, no man could feel safe within his own home.

One man who was certainly not safe within his own home was eighty-two-year old Samuel Churchill, whose wife, Catherine, claimed he had suffered a fit and fallen into the fire. Her story began to unravel when a neighbour reported that she had heard Mrs Churchill yelling at her husband, who responded by crying out, 'Murder! Murder!'

An hour after the neighbour had heard the commotion, Catherine was seen drawing attention to herself in the local Ship Inn. Having thus established an alibi, she returned home, only to rush out again moments later to beg a neighbour, George Whatley, to help her husband, who, she said, had fallen into the fire.

---

[f] Mariticide = the murder of a spouse

Whatley hurried to the cottage and found Samuel lying dead with his head half-burnt in the grate, and wounds to his face and hands. Catherine explained his injuries by claiming he had had a fit, but, when a dubious Whatley sent for a doctor and a policeman, they shared his doubts about Catherine's version of events. Seeing spots of blood on her dress and a blood-stained billhook beneath a chair, the policeman arrested her and charged her with murder.

She stood trial at the Taunton Assizes, where her barrister produced a spirited defence, claiming that she had no motive for murder; and showing that, since the billhook was used to slaughter animals, the blood could be that of a rabbit or a pig. The prosecution, however, easily countered the first argument by demonstrating that money was her overriding motive.

Before marrying the widowed Samuel, Catherine worked as his housekeeper and it was rumoured that, despite a twenty-seven-year age difference, they were having an affair. Whether she was more attracted to the man or to his money is open to question but, when they married in 1871, Samuel was in his seventy-fifth year at a time when the average life expectancy was seventy. As his chief beneficiary, Catherine had every reason to believe that it would not be long before she received a substantial inheritance.

To her chagrin, eight years passed and, as Samuel seemed perfectly healthy, Catherine was often heard to remark that she wished that he were dead. Her frustration simmered until March 1879, when she mistakenly believed that he had changed his will to leave everything to his daughter by his first marriage. Furious that her plans had been thwarted and she had wasted eight years of her life, she flew at him with the billhook and beat him to death.

Even opponents of capital punishment felt that justice had been served when Catherine Churchill was hanged in Taunton Prison on 26th May 1879. Her appalling crime, however, paled in comparison to that of Margaret Walber, who, fourteen years later, subjected her husband to months of abuse before murdering him in a drunken frenzy.

Throughout the nineteenth century, a lack of clean drinking water and the availability of cheap spirits led to such an increase in alcoholism that it was estimated that sixty-four percent of rapes and up to eighty-per-cent of murders were committed while the culprits were intoxicated[11]. The problem was so widespread that it became a common theme in the works of artists, lyricists and writers. George Cruickshank's series of engravings, *The Bottle*, depicted a family man's decline into violence and madness; while Anne Bronte's *The Tenant of Wildfell Hall* included a detailed description of alcohol addiction, probably based on that of the author's brother[g].

> "His appetite for the stimulus of wine had increased upon him, as I had too well foreseen. It was now something more to him than an accessory to social enjoyment: it was an important source of enjoyment in itself. In this time of weakness and depression he would have made it his medicine and support, his comforter, his recreation, and his friend…"[12]

Dickens, too, populated his novels with alcoholic characters, from Sarah Gamp, the hapless nurse in *Martin Chuzzlewit*, to Stephen Blackpool's 'disabled, drunken' wife in *Hard Times*. An entire essay in *Sketches by Boz* was devoted to 'The Drunkard's Death', where the subject was afflicted by:

> "…That fierce rage for the slow, sure poison, that oversteps every other consideration; that casts aside wife, children, friends, happiness, and station; and

---

[g] Branwell Bronte was an alcoholic and opium addict, whose addictions contributed to his early death at the age of thirty.

hurries its victims madly on to degradation and death."[13]

Various efforts were made to combat the problem. Philanthropists built model villages to provide comfortable homes for their workers on condition that they avoided all vices including alcohol. In the cities, Temperance Societies, urged working class men to 'take the pledge' to abstain from drinking, using sentimental songs such as *Father's A Drunkard and Mother Is Dead*; and *Father, Dear Father, Come Home With Me Now*, to press their message home. In Leeds, a Baptist minister, Reverend Jabez Tunnicliff, believing that prevention is better than cure, founded the *Band of Hope* in which children took the pledge. '...Your pledge will bless the world in which you live, and save you from many a sorrow and many a sin,'[14] he told the children; and writing later explained that, 'our only hope of making the world sober was in getting the children on our side.'[15]

Sadly, the efforts of the Temperance Societies and philanthropists had minimal impact on a problem which neither politicians nor legislation seemed able to solve. In 1872, the Prime Minister, William Gladstone, introduced the Licencing Act to enable magistrates to limit opening hours and to close down public houses where drinking was deemed excessive but, when he attempted to increase the duty on beers and spirits, his Bill was defeated in Parliament, leading to the collapse of his Government.

Among the thousands of alcoholics living in nineteenth century Liverpool was a self-employed French polisher, John Walber, and his fifty-three-year-old wife, Margaret, who worked in a local shop. To supplement their income, they took in paid lodgers, who often witnessed their heated arguments, most of which stemmed from Margaret's violent and obsessive jealousy in the face of John's persistent pursuit of other women.

In 1893, they had been married for about five years when Margaret heard that one of John's former girlfriends,

Ann Connelly, had moved into the area. Convinced that he intended to resume the liaison, she began to follow him whenever he left home and, one summer evening, she saw him enter Ann Connelly's house. Rather than confronting him directly, she waited until he returned home and, when he had drunk himself senseless, she dragged him upstairs to the attic, stripped him naked, chained him to the wall and bolted the door.

For four months, he remained naked and chained in the attic and, although the lodgers could hear his cries, not one of them saw fit to intervene. Even when Margaret told them that she was going to buy fly papers[h], they made no effort to rescue the desperate prisoner.

Eventually, word of his situation reached John's sister, but, when she confronted Margaret about it, she replied frankly that she had locked him up to prevent him from frequenting brothels. His sister recommended asking a priest to talk with him, but Margaret said that was not necessary as she had everything in hand.

On 16th November 1893, the lodgers were alarmed by a sudden escalation in the cries and crashing echoing from the floor above. Even this, though, did not impel them to find out what was happening and, when the noise eventually died down, they all continued as though nothing untoward had happened. Soon afterwards, John Murray, Margaret's son by a previous marriage, arrived at the house to speak to his mother. He found her intoxicated in the attic, surrounded by the fragments of a shattered chamber pot; blood-drenched linen; and the corpse of her husband.

When Murray fled in terror, Margaret calmly walked downstairs and told one of the lodgers that her son had killed her husband. When, however, Detective Inspector Blyson appeared on the scene, she confessed that Murray was innocent, and that she was the killer. John, she

---

[h] As fly papers contained arsenic, the implication was that she intended to poison him. See Chapter 3

explained, had found some clothes and, as he intended to leave the house, she had had to kill him to prevent him from visiting prostitutes. She was, she added, so drunk at the time that she hardly knew what she was doing.

At the opening of the trial in St George's Hall on 14th March 1894, the judge, Mr Justice Day, expressed his disbelief and disgust that, in a thriving city like Liverpool, a man could be held prisoner for four months without coming to the attention of the authorities. Suitably reprimanded, the lodgers presented damning evidence against Margaret, while her barrister's sole defence was that, although she had struck her husband, there was no proof that the blow had killed him.

After only fifteen minutes, the jury returned a guilty verdict and, on 2nd April 1894, Margaret became the last woman to be hanged in Liverpool.

# Chapter 3 – The Most Pernicious & Fatal Consequences

Catherine Churchill and Margaret Walber were unusual in that they used physical force to dispose of unwanted husbands. The majority of mariticidal wives preferred to use poison, as it not only required less physical strength but also improved the chances of avoiding detection.

Victorian homes were filled with a myriad of toxins from insecticides and rodenticides to cleaning fluids and medicines, all of which could be purchased cheaply without arousing suspicion. By the middle of the century, one such poison, vitriol – or sulphuric acid that was commonly used as a bleach – had acquired a less salubrious function than that for which it was intended. Newspapers carried lurid accounts of the effects of 'vitriolage', or acid-throwing, in which the unfortunate victims suffered burns to their eyes and other excruciating disfigurements. The renowned forensic toxicologist, Alfred Swaine Taylor, described a case in which:

> "…the evidence proved that a woman had poured oil of vitriol down the throat of her husband while he was lying asleep with his mouth open. She was convicted of the murder. In another case, a woman killed her husband by pouring a solution of corrosive sublimate down his throat while he was sleeping."[16]

Due to its corrosive effects, it was virtually impossible to administer vitriol without arousing suspicion, but the same was not true of arsenic, which was far and away the most popular choice of Victorian poisoners. Odourless, colourless and tasteless, it could be concealed in sugar, flour or salt; or added directly to the food and drink of an unsuspecting victim. Moreover, it was everywhere in a typical Victorian home, being used in clothing, candles, paints, wallpaper, toys and stuffed animals.

"Bird-stuffers," Charles Dickens warned in 1855, "never use arsenical or mercurial preparations to protect the skins you stuff against the voracity of insects. It is fraught with the most pernicious and fatal consequences to yourselves and to the collectors and curators of museums of natural history."[17]

Women who wished to follow the fashion for pale, almost transparent skin could buy 'Arsenic Complexion Wafers', which were advertised as 'harmless' in numerous ladies' journals; or create their own skin lotions using arsenic, cream and cucumber. British troops serving in Africa used arsenic to repel the tsetse fly that spread sleeping sickness; and travellers, including Charles Darwin, believed it was helpful in alleviating eczema and scabies.

One of the most ubiquitous arsenical compounds was Scheele's green, which was used as a dye in wallpapers and paints. The toxic substance not only emitted fumes, which gradually poisoned the household, but could also be accidentally consumed. In one case, a man died when his servant added Scheele's green to a blancmange to give it a more vivid colour, believing it 'was nothing more than an extract of spinach'[18]; and, elsewhere, a baker painted his shelves with Scheele's green, which was absorbed into the warm loaves that he innocently sold to his customers. Even when the noxious nature of the substance had been established, it continued to be sold well into the 1870s.

The most common reason for buying arsenic was for use as a rodenticide, as rats, mice and bed bugs were the scourge of Victorian homes. From the lowliest hovels to the kitchens of Buckingham Palace, the problem was so widespread that Queen Victoria employed an official rat-catcher, Jack Black, who advertised himself as 'rat and mole destroyer to her Majesty.' Mills and factories used specifically-bred dogs such as West Highland and Yorkshire Terriers to deal with vermin, but the average householder used a toxic combination of mercury and white arsenic. Sachets of sufficient strength to kill fifty people could be purchased for a penny, and, until the Arsenic Act of 1851, chemists were not obliged to keep records of how much they sold or to whom.

Would-be killers not only had easy access to the poison but, with patience, they could also ensure that the crime would go undetected. If arsenic were ingested in small quantities over several weeks, it produced symptoms which mimicked those of many common illnesses: congestion, tingling in the extremities, blotchy skin, diarrhoea and vomiting. Eventually, it led to excruciating pain in the digestive tract, which was often misdiagnosed as cholera or dysentery, with the result that many doctors certified murder victims as having died of natural causes. Even if foul play were suspected, it was virtually impossible to prove without physical evidence as, in the early years of Queen Victoria's reign, there was no method of detecting the presence of arsenic *post mortem*.

In 1841, however, the German physician, Hugo Reinsch, devised a test, which would be the undoing of many a murderer. The test involved dissolving the stomach or gut contents in hydrochloric acid, and inserting a strip of copper into the solution. If arsenic, mercury or antimony were present, the copper became coated in a greyish-black film.

It is highly unlikely that forty-two-year-old Sarah Westwood had ever heard of Hugo Reinsch when she decided to murder her nail-maker husband, John. The couple had been married for almost twenty years, during which time Sarah had given birth to numerous children, seven of whom had survived. They all lived together in Shropshire in a small house, which they shared with a lodger, Samuel Phillips, with whom Sarah was having an affair.

John's suspicions about the liaison led to many violent arguments and, on one occasion, when he and Phillips were brawling in public, Sarah was heard viciously urging her lover to kill her husband. Two months later, she decided to take undertake that task herself.

Claiming that her children were suffering from scabies, she bought a sachet of arsenic from a chemist, who had no reason to suspect her malevolent intentions. After all, arsenic was a safer treatment than the sulphuric acid in which a workhouse child had been bathed the previous year in an horrendous attempt to combat the same condition

On 9th November 1843, John Westwood came home from work at lunchtime and, after eating a bowl of gruel, he was struck with violent stomach pains and vomiting. Throughout the afternoon, his symptoms intensified, but he refused Sarah's offer to fetch a doctor and, at nine o'clock that night, he breathed his last.

The sudden onset of his illness and the speed of his demise prompted the coroner to order a post-mortem, during which the Reinsch Test revealed the presence of large quantities of arsenic in his stomach. Despite her vehement protests, Sarah was charged with murder and sent for trial at the Stafford Assizes. The most telling evidence came from her own children, who innocently stated that they had never had scabies; but admitted having seen a white powder in the gruel that their mother fed their father.

Sarah was found guilty and sentenced to hang, but, in spite of their apparent betrayal, she felt no animosity towards her daughters. When the youngest girls visited her in prison shortly before her execution, their cries were so heart-rending that reports of the incident prompted calls for the abolition of the death penalty for mothers.

On the day of the execution, Sarah's courage failed and, as she approached the gallows, her legs gave way and she was unable to stand. The hangman, George Smith, brought a stool for her to sit on, as he placed the noose around her neck and dispatched her into oblivion.

The news accounts of a pathetic young woman fainting in fear at the scaffold gave impetus to the opponents of capital punishment, who reiterated that hanging failed to serve as a deterrent. Over the next few years, they found further evidence to support that claim as, in spite of the threat of execution, numerous wives followed Sarah's example and poisoned their husbands.

When twenty-eight-year-old Thomas Ball was suddenly afflicted with griping pains after eating a bowl of gruel, his wife, Mary, summoned a Dr Prouse, who diagnosed inflammation of the bowels – a not uncommon condition for navvies[i] like Thomas, whose strenuous labours often resulted in hernias or 'ruptures'. Prouse prescribed something soothing but Thomas continued to deteriorate and, less than forty-eight hours later, on 20th May 1849, Mary sent word to the doctor that, 'Poor Tom is dead.'

Although Prouse was happy to confirm that his patient had died of natural causes, neighbours began to gossip about the violent rows that had characterised the Balls' marriage. Their life together had not been happy as all but one of their twelve children had died in infancy, and, while Thomas was a notoriously heavy drinker and womaniser, Mary regularly escaped to the arms of a neighbour, William Bacon.

When the gossip reached the ears of an experienced officer, Constable Haddon, he asked a colleague, Vernon, to accompany him to Mary's home to question her about her husband's death. She readily admitted buying arsenic to kill bed bugs, but dismissed the suggestion that Thomas

---

[i] Navvies (short for 'navigators') were labourers who built the railways and canals.

had been poisoned. Moments later, she changed her mind and said it was possible that he had mistaken arsenic for salt; and, when pressed for more details, she admitted that, when he had asked her for a purgative, she had mixed a few grains of arsenic with salt.

She was arrested and taken into custody, pending a post-mortem, which revealed a potentially fatal quantity of arsenic in the deceased's stomach. Charged with murder, Mary was detained for a further two months before standing trial at the Coventry Assizes.

Judge Taylor Coleridge – a nephew of the romantic poet, Samuel Coleridge – presided over the proceedings, during which the prosecution made much of the contradictory accounts that Mary had given to Haddon and Vernon. Neighbours testified that she had always disliked her husband; and Judge Coleridge appeared more shocked by her adultery than by the murder. When the jury returned a guilty verdict but added a plea for mercy, Coleridge remarked that there were no grounds for clemency as the prisoner was obviously 'evil'.

Whether or not she was evil, an over-zealous prison chaplain, Richard Chapman, was determined to save her soul. As she awaited execution, he warned her that, unless she repented and made a full confession, she would endure hell fire and eternal damnation. To give her a foretaste of what to expect, he held her arm over a candle flame until her skin blistered and she screamed in pain. Hearing the commotion, the shocked wardresses reported the matter to the governor, who, in turn, informed a magistrate who happened to be visiting the prison. On being questioned, the unrepentant Chapman insisted that a few minutes' suffering was nothing if it saved the sinner from eternal damnation, but the magistrate did not share his zeal and arranged for him to be permanently removed from his duties.

In spite of his unorthodox methods, Chapman's warnings persuaded Mary to make a full confession. She admitted that she had deliberately mixed arsenic into the salt, knowing that Thomas would add it to his gruel. She regretted what she had done, she said, and wished that, instead of killing her husband, she had left him and thrown herself on the mercy of the workhouse. The next day, a crowd of twenty-thousand people gathered to watch her execution – the last public hanging in Coventry.

As Haddon understood, gossip could prove very useful in casting light upon crimes, particularly in close-knit communities where neighbours kept a close eye on each other's business. Tittle-tattle provided investigators with a wealth of information, and nothing was more likely to set the gossips' tongues a-wagging than a recently bereaved widow moving on with unseemly haste to a new lover.

When Thomas Harris died in the spring of 1850, no one suspected anything untoward until two weeks later when his fifty-six-year old widow, Hannah, remarried.

'Only two weeks!' the gossips went wild. 'Poor Thomas body was barely cold…and hadn't Hannah behaved strangely during his final illness?'

She had blithely said that she would not remain a widow for long, suggesting that she had already planned to marry the local shoemaker, John Curtis. When the busybodies learned that she had accepted Curtis' proposal on the very day that Thomas died, the furore reached fever-pitch and came to the attention of coroner, who ordered an exhumation.

Mr Herepath of Bristol University analysed the remains and found traces of arsenic in Thomas' viscera. Further inquiries revealed that the deceased had been perfectly well until mid-April, when his health suddenly declined very rapidly. Within a week, he was emaciated and unable to walk unaided; and he had been seen vomiting blood.

Hannah did not deny that she had purchased arsenic but claimed to have done so at Thomas' request in order to poison rats; and, when she heard that the poison had been found in her late husband stomach, she suggested that he had taken it accidentally, mistaking it for bicarbonate of soda.

It took under an hour for the jury at the Gloucester Assizes to find her guilty of murder, leaving the judge no option but to sentence her to death. Petitions were sent to the Home Secretary, George Grey, arguing that there was no evidence that Hannah had administered the poison, as a result of which, he commuted her sentence to life imprisonment.

Although, at the time, Grey's decision was seen as merciful, it raises a serious question: if there were insubstantial evidence that she was guilty of murder, why was she not acquitted?

Hannah accepted her lot with good grace and, on being transferred to the Millbank in London, she became a model prisoner, endearing herself to the wardresses and acting as a mother to her fellow inmates. She was, wrote the prison matron:

> "A tall, grey-haired woman, looking older than her years, bent nearly double, and leaning on a stick; a woman with a kind, motherly face...A prisoner one took naturally to, and for whom I felt almost unconsciously the respect due from youth to age, until the nature of the crime sent all reverential feeling to the background."

Throughout her sentence, she continued to insist that she was innocent although she seemed to enjoy prison life, which she described as 'very comfortable'. When she became feebler, she was transferred to the nursery wing, where she enjoyed caring for the prisoners' children and giving advice to the young mothers.

After more than a decade, she expressed a desire to end her days among her friends and relations, and, in view of her good conduct, the Home Secretary granted her a pardon, enabling her to die a free woman.

Such a fate would surely have appealed to twenty-seven-year-old Sarah Ann French, who would have been happy to have her sentence commuted from death to penal servitude. Instead, though, petitions for mercy were to no avail and the desperate woman went screaming to the gallows.

According to their neighbours in the East Sussex village of Chiddingly, William and Sarah Ann French were a cheerful and loving couple. For almost ten years they lived contentedly together, raising a young son and creating the impression of happy and devoted family until Sarah Ann became infatuated with her sister's boyfriend, twenty-year-old James Hickson.

Although they often spent time together when her husband was working, Hickson soundly rejected Sarah Ann's amorous advances because she was married. Teasingly, she asked him if he would feel differently if she were single, and, when he gave a vague reply, she told him that William was often ill and could die at any moment.

Shortly before Christmas 1851, she redoubled her efforts to woo him, telling him she that she had £500 in savings and, if her husband were dead, she would marry him and keep him in such comfort that he would never have to work again. Flattered as he was, Hickson did not take her promises seriously, as thirty-five-year-old William was a strong and healthy farm labourer, who was nothing like the sickly man that Sarah Ann had described.

Although she clearly relished the thought of freeing herself from her husband, there is nothing to suggest that she would have taken steps to hasten his demise had he himself not placed too great a temptation into her hands. Returning from work, William bought a packet of arsenic to kill vermin, and asked Sarah Ann to keep it safe and out of the reach of their little boy. On Christmas Eve, his brother visited and found him in excellent health but that evening Sarah Ann fed him an onion pie, after which he complained of a headache and nausea.

The following week, as he had several bouts of vomiting, Sarah Ann told friends that she had heard something rupture inside him, implying that he had a hernia. She did not, however, think it sufficiently serious to call a doctor, even when New Year came and went and he showed no signs of improvement.

Shortly before midnight on 7th January 1852, Sarah Ann called out to a neighbour that she feared William was dead. The neighbour sent for an assistant surgeon, who confirmed that life was indeed extinct but, when furnished with the details of William's decline, he expressed great astonishment that Sarah Ann had not sought medical help. Nonetheless, she appeared suitably grief-stricken and, as a post-mortem revealed nothing untoward, the inquest recorded that death was due to natural causes.

There, the story might have ended had Sarah Ann not been so eager to invite Hickson into her bed. Within days of William's death, neighbours gossiped about the cheerful widow and her young lover and, when the rumours reached the ears of a police superintendent, he expressed concern to the coroner about safety of the inquest verdict. The coroner ordered an exhumation in preparation for second inquest, and, this time, when a surgeon from Guy's Hospital performed a post-mortem, he found arsenic in the stomach and intestine.

In March 1852, Sarah Ann stood on trial for murder at the Lewes Assizes, where she desperately tried to save her neck by blaming Hickson for the crime. She falsely accused him of having tried to put poison into William's milk, and said that he had often threatened to kill him so that he could marry her. Her barrister added weight to her statement by suggesting that the promise of £500 gave Hickson a motive for murder, whereas Sarah Ann had nothing to gain from her husband's death.

When questioned, Hickson, horrified by the accusation, told the court that Sarah Ann had initiated their liaison and that she had asked him to marry her on the day of William's funeral. Less enamoured than she was, he had replied that it was too soon after William's death, and told her that they should wait for at least a year.

The jury was divided about whose account to believe and, after lengthy deliberations, failed to reach a unanimous verdict. The majority, however, was convinced of Sarah Ann's guilt, and consequently the judges passed the death sentence. In the days leading up to her execution, Sarah Ann had plenty of time to reflect on what she had done. She knew only too well what to expect from the hangman, for, three years earlier she had witnessed the execution of another husband-killer, Mary Ann Geering[j]. On the morning of 10th April 1852, Sarah Ann made a full confession to the chaplain of Lewes Prison, and, in a state of near collapse, she was handed over to William Calcraft, in a front of a crowd of four thousand people.

Fourteen years later, Calcraft, was called upon to dispatch another seemingly happily married woman, who had likewise poisoned her husband – who was also named William – to replace him with a younger and rather reluctant lover.

In 1866, William and Mary Ann Ashford had been married for two decades and, although they were childless, they seemed perfectly happy together in their comfortable home in Clyst Honiton near Exeter. Six years earlier, William, a successful shoemaker, had taken on a young

[j] See Chapter 14

apprentice, Frank Pratt, who was only a child in 1860 but, four years later, he had grown into a handsome young man whose youthful physique and good looks did not escape Mary Ann's attention.

In spite of a twenty-year age difference, the couple began an affair, which came to an abrupt end when William discovered what was happening. He angrily threw Frank out of his house, and wrote a will, making his father his sole beneficiary, leaving his unfaithful wife nothing.

As soon as his anger cooled, he relented. He altered the will to leave everything to Mary Ann and even allowed Frank Pratt to return to work for him as a journeyman shoemaker[k]. Such generosity and forgiveness brought Frank to his senses and, when Mary Ann attempted to resume their affair, he rejected her advances, insisting he would not repay his employer's kindness with deception.

Spurned and frustrated, Mary Ann watched her former lover enjoying the company of younger women, until, burning with resentment, she convinced herself that only her husband's death would help her to regain his affection. Callously, she considered her options and, realising that a sudden death would arouse suspicion, she decided to poison William gradually by lacing his meals with small quantities of arsenic and strychnine.

The effects of strychnine are even more horrendous than those of arsenic. Initially it causes stiffness in the joints and soreness in the muscles, which intensify into severe muscle spasms, resulting in fit-like jerking movements until the muscles of the airways are paralysed and the victim dies of asphyxiation.

On 29th October 1865, William suffered a bout of diarrhoea, which he treated with a jalap purgative and, by the following morning, he had fully recovered. Two days

---

[k] A journeyman is a skilled worker who has completed an apprenticeship but is not sufficiently experienced to work independently as a Master Craftsman.

later, his symptoms returned more severely and, to divert suspicion from herself, Mary Ann sought the advice of a physician, Dr Roberts, on how best to treat him.

For the next few days, William continued to deteriorate and, on 2nd November, he sent word to the doctor asking him to visit. Roberts was so baffled by his symptoms and his failure to respond to treatment that he asked his colleague, Dr Miles, for a second opinion. Miles was equally mystified as to the cause of William's excruciating pains, and, when he died on 3rd November, both doctors insisted upon a post-mortem.

Mr Herepath, the chemist who had given evidence at the trial of Hannah Curtis, analysed William's stomach and liver and found quantities of poison; and several witnesses reported having seen blue and white powders in the vessels from which Mary Ann had fed him. These, too, were examined and found to contain arsenic and strychnine, as did Mary Ann's purse and handkerchief. When the police arrived to arrest her, she further incriminated herself by hurriedly throwing a packet of powder into the fire.

The jury at the Exeter Lenten Assizes took only ten minutes to find her guilty of murder; and, in view of the callousness of her crime, there was widespread public support when the judge pronounced the death sentence. Mary Ann, though, was determined to avoid the gallows and, on being returned to the prison, she attempted, unsuccessfully, to strangle herself with a handkerchief.

Up to twenty-thousand people turned out to watch the hanging, during which, thanks to Calcraft's incompetence, Mary Ann was left writhing at the end of the rope for three full minutes. In spite of the horrendous spectacle of a woman being asphyxiated, the crowd had little sympathy with a wife who had inflicted such an agonising death on her innocent and forgiving husband.

# Chapter 4 – Means, Motive & Opportunity

The Reinsch Test could prove that a victim had been poisoned but science alone could not detect who was responsible for the murder. When deciding between a number of suspects, therefore, the police relied heavily on 'the rule of three': who had the means, the motive and the opportunity to commit the crime?

This method had severe limitations as, in some cases, several suspects fit the rule; and in other cases, the accused might have the means and opportunity, but detectives struggled to find a motive for murder. Such was the case of seventeen-year-old Catherine Morley, who, in October 1846, ignoring her mother's warnings that she was too young to make such a commitment, left her job as a housemaid to marry her childhood friend, a farm labourer, John Foster.

Immediately after the wedding, the couple moved in with Catherine's mother in Sudbury, but, three days later, with John's permission, Catherine went to stay with an aunt in Pakenham and did not return home for over a week. For the next fortnight, the newly-weds seemed quite happy together, but, on 17th November, after eating some dumplings which Catherine had made, John was violently sick and spent the rest of the night retching. Catherine scraped up the remains of the dumplings and fed them to the hens in the yard, and, by the following afternoon, all the chickens were dead – as was her husband.

A surgeon, Mr Jones, initially believed that John had died of cholera but when a post-mortem revealed a substantial quantity of arsenic in his stomach, Catherine was arrested and sent for trial at the Suffolk Assizes in March 1847.

Her barrister's sole defence was that she had no reason to kill her husband, and that public opinion was so against her that she could not receive a fair hearing. The prosecution's case was far stronger, and, after only fifteen minutes, the jury found her guilty of wilful murder. The following day, the judge, Baron Pollock, choked back his tears as he sentenced her to hang, but Catherine stood stoically in the dock, displaying no emotion.

> "Not a single tear glistened in her eye, which was unobservant and inattentive," wrote a journalist who was present in the court. "Not a single contraction of the facial muscles betokened the inward workings of suppressed feelings but calm and composed she received the sentence as she had listened to the overwhelming evidence adduced against her, and she descended from the dock to the dark cell beneath with as light a step as if she had been convicted on an ordinary crime."

She was taken to Bury St Edmunds Gaol, where she signed a full confession, stating that she had acted alone and had purchased arsenic to poison her husband three days before she killed him. He was a good man who had always been kind to her, she said, and her only explanation for the murder was that, 'I never had any affection for him, and wished to go back into service.'[19]

After thanking the prison staff and the chaplain, she added:

> "I do not wish to live, for I never could be happy in this world, and I hope. through the merits and blood of my Saviour, and a sincere repentance of this and all my sins, to obtain forgiveness of God, and to be received into Heaven. I die at peace with all, having no complaint to make of any witness that appeared against me on my trial, and full of remorse for the crime which brings me to this premature death."[20]

At nine o'clock in the morning on 17th April 1847, she walked bravely and silently to the gallows where over ten thousand people were waiting to watch her hang. She swung on the rope for two minutes before breathing her last.

The following day, newspaper articles complained about the behaviour of the crowds and spread the false rumour that Catherine's death had been particularly gruesome. The vivid and erroneous descriptions led to a debate in the House of Lords, where it was left to the Marquess of Lansdowne to assure his fellow peers that the execution had been carried out with 'greatest propriety and solemnity, and that the unfortunate person did not undergo a greater degree of suffering than what necessarily belonged to the infliction of the punishment to which she had been sentenced.'[21] In an early reference to 'fake news', the Marquess added that it was as well to remember that not everything that appears in the press is true.

The Foster case was tragic due to the youth of both the victim and killer, and the lack of a genuine motive for the crime. Even more tragic, though, were the cases of two completely innocent women, who had the motive, means and opportunity to kill and were consequently hanged for crimes they did not commit.

In 1868, when Priscilla Biggadyke stood in the dock at the Lincoln Assizes charged with the murder of her husband, she had such faith in the law that she had no doubt she would be acquitted and the real murderer would be found. Even when the jury found her guilty and the judge sentenced her to hang, she remained cheerfully confident that the truth would be discovered and she would be reprieved.

There was no doubt that her labourer husband, Richard, had died of arsenic poisoning; nor that, as the prosecution claimed, she had a motive to kill him. At the time of his death, she was having an affair with a lodger, Thomas Proctor, who shared a tiny one-bedroomed cottage with Richard and Priscilla, their three children, and another lodger, George Ironside. According to the prosecution, Richard's discovery of the affair gave Priscilla a motive to kill him; and she had the opportunity to do so, as she made all his meals. One evening in late September, she gave him tea and home-made cake, after which he began retching and vomiting. A doctor was summoned but was unable to find the cause of the illness, and, by dawn, Richard was dead.

When a post-mortem revealed a large quantity of arsenic in the deceased's stomach, Priscilla informed the police that she had seen Proctor adding a white powder to Richard's tea. The fact that Proctor was a rat-catcher with access to a variety of poisons, made this claim feasible, but, rather than exonerating Priscilla, it convinced the police that she and her lover had colluded with one other to dispose of her husband.

Both were arrested and charged with murder but, when the trial opened in Lincoln, the judge inexplicably declared that Proctor had no case to answer and ordered his immediate release.

After the trial, Priscilla was taken to the execution cell in Lincoln Castle, where she naively assured her visitors that the truth would soon be discovered and she would be released. Not until the morning of her execution, did she realise that her optimism had been unfounded, and, when the wardresses came to lead her to the gallows, she fainted in fright and had to be carried.

As the hangman, George Askern, tied her hands, she gasped, 'Shame on you! You're not going to hang me?'

At the last moment, the chaplain pleaded with her to make a full confession but she remained silent. The incompetent Askern added to the horror by letting the knot of the noose rest beneath her chin, resulting in a slow and agonising strangulation.

Two years later, Thomas Proctor lay on his deathbed when, suddenly overcome by the fear of eternal damnation, he admitted that he had poisoned Richard Biggadyke and allowed an innocent woman to hang.

A truly bizarre coincidence occurred sixteen years later when Priscilla's friend, forty-nine-year-old Mary Leffley, stood in the same dock at the Lincoln Assizes, wrongly charged with an identical crime.

Mary had lived with her husband, William, on a small farm in Lincolnshire, and it was widely known that theirs was not a happy marriage. When William died after eating a rice pudding that Mary had made for him, she was immediately suspected of his murder. His stomach contained enough arsenic to kill fifty people and, when the case came to trial, the jury took little more than half an hour to find Mary guilty.

Despite her vehement protestations of innocence, she was sentenced to hang, and the recently-appointed James Berry was chosen to carry out the execution. Like Priscilla, she was so convinced that she would obtain a reprieve that, when Berry entered the execution cell, she clung to her bed, refusing to move.

> "She was in a nervous, agitated state," Berry wrote, "praying to God for salvation, not as a murderess but as an innocent woman. On my approach she threw up her hands and shrieked, 'Murder! Murder!' and she had to be led to the scaffold by two female warders, shrieking wildly all the time She died as she had lived, impenitent and untruthful, denying her guilt to the last."[22]

Berry was mistaken, for Mary was telling the truth. Some years later, a local farmer on his deathbed admitted that he had been angry with William Leffley and, while Mary was not looking, he had entered her cottage and sprinkled arsenic into the rice pudding.

Priscilla Biggadyke and Mary Leffley were vindicated within a few years of their executions, but a far more controversial case is that of Florence Maybrick, who, for over a century, has divided opinion about whether or not she murdered her husband.

In 1880, James Maybrick, a prosperous cotton merchant, was returning to his native Liverpool from a business trip to the United States, when he made the acquaintance of eighteen-year-old Florence Chandler, an American 'southern belle' from Alabama. Forty-three-year-old James was instantly drawn to Florence's zest and youthful allure; and, to his delight, the attraction was mutual. By the time the ship docked in England, they were engaged and, less than twelve months later, they were married in the fashionable St James' Church in London's Piccadilly.

Over the next few years, Florence gave birth to two children, James and Gladys, before the family eventually settled into the imposing Battlecrease House in Aigburth – a leafy suburb of Liverpool. To the outside world, they appeared to live a charmed life, moving in the most fashionable circles, and enjoying all the benefits of middle-class opulence.

Behind the façade, however, all was not well in the Maybrick household, as, once the first heady rush of romance had faded, the couple discovered that they barely knew one another and had very little in common. James was disappointed to learn that Florence did not possess a fortune as he had been led to believe, and he was irked by her expensive tastes and lack of financial acumen.

For her part, Florence was humiliated when he drastically reduced her housekeeping; and was shocked to discover that he was a fearful hypochondriac, addicted to numerous medications, including arsenic, for his many imaginary ailments. Far from being the kindly and sophisticated gentleman that she had envisaged, he was dull, obsessively jealous and prone to angry outbursts. Most woundingly of all, she learned that he had four illegitimate children by a long-time mistress, to whom he continued to send regular payments. In retaliation, she refused to share his bed, but instead found solace in the arms of several lovers, including her brother-in-law, Edwin Maybrick, and James' friend and fellow cotton-merchant, Alfred Brierley.

By the spring of 1889, James' addictions were affecting his behaviour, making him so erratic that Florence pleaded with his doctors to help him. When nothing was done, she wrote to his brother, Michael[1], in London, advising him that James was regularly taking a white powder which she believed to be strychnine.

As Michael also failed to act, Florence persuaded Brierley to spend a weekend with her in London, where she arranged to meet a lawyer to discuss the possibility of a legal separation. In early April, back in Liverpool, she and James attended the Grand National and, at the racetrack they happened to meet Brierley. When the Maybricks returned home, James, angrily accused Florence of flirting with her lover, and struck her so violently that she was left with a black eye. The next day, she poured out her heart to her doctor, telling him that she longed for a separation. The doctor unhelpfully replied that such a course was unwise, and advised her instead to seek a reconciliation with her husband.

A few weeks later, James summoned Dr Humphries to Battlecrease House, complaining of pains in his muscles, twitching in his limbs, and itching in his throat – the typical symptoms of strychnine poisoning. The doctor's treatments were ineffective and, as James continued to deteriorate, his brothers, Michael and Edwin, arrived to take charge of the situation.

Excluding Florence from their discussions, they came to the conclusion that James was being poisoned and,

---

[1] Michael Maybrick was a well-known singer and composer, who, under the pseudonym, Stephen Adams, wrote many popular songs, including the Victorian favourite *The Holy City*.

as Florence was their only suspect, they began to build a case against her. In this, they were aided by the children's nurse, Alice Yapp, who pointed out that her mistress was in the habit of soaking fly papers to extract the arsenic. More damning still, was Yapp's revelation of the contents of a letter that Florence had written to Brierley. According to the nursemaid, Mrs Maybrick had asked her to post the letter but, on the way to the post box, she had 'accidentally' dropped it in some mud. As the envelope was sullied, she took it home to replace it, and, in doing so, she 'happened to' notice that Florence had written that she expected James' imminent demise.

This news so disturbed Michael Maybrick that, when James died on May 11th, he placed his sister-in-law under house arrest while he and Edwin searched through every drawer and cupboard, finding several supplies of arsenic as well as a collection of incriminating letters to Florence from three separate lovers.

Alone and friendless, Florence wrote desperately to Brierley:

> "I am writing to you to give me every assistance in your power in my present fearful trouble. I am in custody, without any of my family with me at present, and without money. I have cabled to my solicitor in New York to come to me at once. In the meantime, send some money for present needs. The truth is known about my visit to London, and your last letter is in the hands of the police. Appearances are terribly against me; but before God, I swear I am innocent."[23]

On Michael's insistence, a post-mortem was performed, which revealed only that James had died from severe gastro-enteritis, with insufficient evidence to confirm that this was caused by poison. His body was released for burial but, soon after the funeral, the coroner, at the behest of the Maybrick brothers, ordered an exhumation so that the organs could be removed for a more thorough analysis.

"This searching a body for arsenic after exhumation," wrote one contemporary commentator, "is not always an entirely satisfactory proceeding, because arsenic is such a common thing – it is found in so many things, lead, copper, dyed paper, clothes, glass, indeed, in almost everything, though it is never found in the tissues of the human body unless it has been introduced into them from without: still, cases have been known where arsenic has got into coffins and graves from the copper nails and other accompaniments of interment, and even, I believe, in one recorded case, from the soil itself. In the well-known Loughton case in Essex, in 1878, Dr Tidy found no less than 6 grains of arsenic in the viscera of an exhumed body; the arsenic had not been taken by the deceased at all, but had come from some violet powder which had been dusted over the corpse."[24]

Only a tiny amount of arsenic was discovered in James' remains, and, considering that he was in the habit of taking the substance as a medication, there was clearly insufficient medical evidence to charge Florence with murder. The incriminating letters, however, painted a different picture, showing her not only as an adulteress but also as a woman who was desperate to be free from her husband.

After a series of Police Court hearings, Florence was committed for trial at the Liverpool Assizes, where she would be represented by the diligent and able Sir Charles Russell. By then, though, the press had sensationalised the story, portraying James as the innocent victim of a wicked, unfaithful wife.

"The excitement ran so high," she wrote, "that the Liverpool crowds even hissed me as I was driven through the streets. It was a mockery of justice to hold such a trial in such a place as Liverpool, at such a time, by a common jury; and it was a mockery of common sense to expect that any Liverpool common jury could, when they got into the jury-box, dismiss from their minds all they had heard and seen."[25]

Her request to be tried instead in London was refused, and, when the hearing began on 31st July in St George's Hall, Liverpool, there was so much excitement that refined ladies fought over tickets to the public gallery. Along the crowded benches sat many of Florence's former friends who, much to her dismay, had come not to show support but rather out of a prurient interest in the details of her marriage and affairs. They were suitably aghast when letters from her lovers were read aloud; and the public, like the judge, seemed more shocked by her infidelities than by the alleged murder.

Russell presented a strong defence, pointing out that the fly papers were irrelevant; that James was an addict; and that he had not died of arsenic poisoning. His efforts were severely hampered, though, by the aged judge, James Fitzjames Stephen, whose prejudicial summing up of the case was virtually an order to the jury to find her guilty. Implying that Florence had murdered her husband in order to continue her illicit liaisons, he made it clear that he considered her behaviour disgusting.

"For a person," he told the jury, "to go on deliberately administering poison to a poor, helpless sick man upon whom she has already inflicted a dreadful injury, an injury fateful to married life, the person who could do such a thing as that must indeed be destitute of the least trace of human feeling."[26]

After only forty minutes, the jury returned a guilty verdict, and Stephens donned his black cap to utter the fateful words:

> "The court doth order you to be taken from hence to the place from whence you came, and from thence to the place of execution, and that you be hanged by the neck until you are dead, and that your body be afterward buried within the precincts of the prison in which you shall be confined after your conviction. And may the Lord have mercy upon your soul!"

By then, though, fickle public opinion had swung in Florence's favour and, as she was driven back to Walton Gaol, crowds gathered to cheer her, while the judge was met with hisses and jeers.

Over the next three weeks, petitions poured in from across the country and from Florence's native America; and when the Home Secretary, Henry Matthews, had read through the transcript of the trial, he declared that there was insufficient evidence to prove that she had committed murder. As in Hannah Curtis' case, this should have led to her release, but instead Matthews commuted the sentence to life imprisonment.

Florence was duly taken to Woking Prison, while Russell embarked on a campaign to win a reprieve. Books were written and letters were sent to Queen Victoria, but years passed before it was agreed that her sentence should be reduced to fifteen years. In 1904, she was finally released and retired to a convent in Truro before returning to the United States where, using her maiden name, Florence Chandler, she earned a living giving talks about her story. After two years, she withdrew from public life, and spent the rest of her days in a small shack, surrounded by cats. She died in poverty in 1941, a month after her seventy-ninth birthday.

# Chapter 5 – Not Proven

If Florence Maybrick had been tried in Scotland, she would probably have enjoyed fifteen more years of freedom, as Scottish juries had the option of returning a verdict of 'not proven.' Although this failed to remove all suspicion from defendants, it at least saved them from the gallows or imprisonment, which, in 1844, would prove most advantageous to twenty-five-year-old Christina Gilmour, who almost certainly murdered her husband.

Blessed with good looks, a solid education and a very wealthy father, Christina Cochran had enjoyed a comfortable upbringing in Paisley in Renfrewshire. As soon as she came of age, her charm and elegance attracted several suitors, the most persistent of whom was a farmer's son, John Anderson. It was generally accepted that the couple would marry, and Christina gave John every indication that this was the case, but, when a wealthy farmer, John Gilmour, appeared on the scene, Christina's parents felt that he had better prospects than John Anderson.

Mr and Mrs Cochran encouraged Gilmour to court their daughter, but, when he first proposed, she refused him. Undeterred, he declared that he could not live without her, and, when he threatened to kill himself unless she changed her mind, she yielded. Almost immediately, she realised that she had made a mistake and, as soon as the engagement was announced, she became moody and morose, cancelling the wedding twice before she finally plighted her troth on 29th November 1842.

The newly-weds moved into Gilmour's farm in the village of Inchinnan, where, from the start, it was clear that Christina was not happy. She spent her wedding night sitting up in a chair and, in the weeks that followed, she told John that she would never sleep with him – an announcement that he accepted calmly, possibly believing that things would change when they knew one another better. More surprisingly, she invited her sister to stay but insisted that she took all her meals on her own in the kitchen, so that she and her husband could dine alone together.

A month after the wedding, Christina asked a servant to purchase a packet of arsenic, and, the following day, the same servant saw her throw it into the fire. It would be wrong to use it, Christina said cryptically, adding that she had no idea how it was done anyway.

The next morning, John fell ill with griping pains in his stomach, and, when he visited his father just after New Year, his face was swollen and he vomited several times. His symptoms continued for several days until 5th January when he became so weak that he had to take to his bed. Christina played the dutiful wife, preparing and serving all his meals, but, when the farm hands suggested calling a doctor, she replied that John had an aversion to medications and would not allow it. Disbelieving her explanation, one of the more devoted hands, waited for her to go out before sneaking inside to speak to his master. John was pleased to see him, and appeared even more relieved when he offered to send for Dr M'Laws.

Christina, meanwhile, had gone to visit an uncle, Mr Robinson, whom she had not seen for several years. To his surprise, she asked him for advice about how best to treat her husband's illness, and frankly confessed that she regretted marrying him as she was still in love with John Anderson. The shocked uncle offered to send his own doctor to Inchinnan but Christina repeated that her husband had an aversion to medications and asked her uncle to visit him instead.

The farm hand, meanwhile, had located an inebriate Dr M'Laws, who diagnosed an inflammatory illness, which he treated by bleeding the patient and ordering him to be rubbed with turpentine. When Christina arrived home, she dismissed the drunken doctor, telling him that his services were no longer required.

The following morning, she visited Wylie's chemist shop and, giving her name as Miss Robinson, asked for a packet of arsenic. When Mr Wylie asked her what she wished to use it for, she replied that it was for a farmer, John Fergusson of Paisley, who needed to poison the rats on his farm.

That afternoon, when her uncle arrived at Inchinnan, Christina again complained that she was unhappy in her marriage, but Mr Robinson was far more concerned about her husband's illness. He summoned his own doctor, M'Kenchie, who arrived soon afterwards and, having prescribed a medication to settle John's stomach, asked Christina to preserve specimens of his excreta in the hope of discovering the cause of his illness.

That night, Mr Robinson sat up with the patient to allow Christina a little respite; and, when M'Kenchie returned in the morning, he was pleased to find some improvement. When, though, he asked Christina for the specimens, she replied that there were none. Over the next few days, as she resumed her husband's care, he again deteriorated and, on 11th January, he was convinced that he was dying. He whispered to a farm hand that he wanted a post-mortem; and his nephew, who was also present, heard him plead with Christina to tell him if she had poisoned him.

When he died, Christina returned to her parents' home, and, during her absence from Inchinnan, the servants and farm hands discussed their suspicions. Three months later, their concerns came to the attention of the authorities and, when Mr Cochran heard that they were about to arrest his daughter, he hastily arranged to send her away to America. Without even allowing her time to bid farewell to her mother, he packed her off to Liverpool where one of his acquaintances was waiting to pose as her husband on the voyage to New York.

Back in Renfrewshire, John's body was exhumed on 22nd April, confirming the police's suspicions that he had been poisoned. Christina's parents denied all knowledge of her whereabouts, but, when detectives learned that she had set sail for America, they dispatched officers on a faster Cunard steamer and, by the time that she arrived at Staten Island, they were waiting to arrest her. At first, she claimed that she was not Christina Gilmour, before feigning madness in the hope of avoiding extradition. Consequently, the officers were forced to wait for several weeks until the American authorities deemed her fit to travel, and, by the time that she appeared in the High Court in Edinburgh, her husband had been dead for over a year.

In court, she admitted that she had purchased arsenic but claimed she had planned to use it on herself to escape from her unhappy marriage. She had never, she insisted, administered poison to her husband, and, if he had died of arsenic poisoning, she could only assume that he was equally unhappy and had taken it himself.

In his closing statement for the prosecution, the Lord Advocate asked whether anyone contemplating suicide would choose a lingering and painful death by taking small amounts of poison over several weeks. There was no doubt, he argued, that Christina had obtained arsenic and:

> "...she might have poisoned herself, or she might have poisoned her husband. Her husband is poisoned. She is not. By a most extraordinary chance, the cup which she mixed for herself has not been quaffed by her, but by some unknown and mysterious hand was conveyed to the lips of her husband. Can you, then, doubt the purpose for

which that poison was obtained or the purpose to which it was applied?"

Thomas Maitland for the defence called over a hundred witnesses, who attested to the prisoner's good character and her devotion to her husband. Even if, Maitland argued, her behaviour had given rise to suspicion, the jury must not convict her unless her guilt were proven.

In his summing up, the judge observed that he could see no obvious motive for such a heinous crime, and that, until the time of John's death, Christina's conduct had been exemplary. If, he repeated, the jury had any doubts at all, they could not return a guilty verdict.

When, after an hour's deliberations, the jury returned a verdict of not proven, the court erupted in loud applause. Christina was released and led away through a side door to avoid the waiting journalists and the crowds who had been eagerly anticipating the outcome. She quietly returned to her parents' home where she lived peacefully for the next sixty years, becoming, according to a local clergyman, 'a charming old lady, serene and beautiful, famed throughout the district for her singular piety.'[27]

The verdict, however, had not exonerated her and many questions remain unanswered. Why, if she had no malign intentions, had she given a false name to the chemist and concocted a story about why she required arsenic? Why had she told her uncle and the farm hand that John refused to see a doctor; and why had she ignored M'Kenchie's instructions to save the contents of his stomach?

The not proven verdict probably enabled Christina Gilmour to 'get away with murder'; and it is highly likely that, two years later, Janet M'Lellan was equally fortunate to escape with her life, when she stood on trial for the same crime in the same city.

Janet had never had any intention of remaining faithful to her husband, James M'Lellan – a pious weaver, thirty years her senior. An affair with a lodger resulted in the birth of twins, whom the long-suffering James agreed to raise as his own. His apparent kindness, however, masked a self-righteous resentment and each evening, during family prayers, he pointedly prayed aloud for forgiveness for Janet's sins. His preaching became so incessant that, one evening, she seized an axe and threatened to kill him.

The moment passed but, in the summer of 1844, James was violently sick after eating a breakfast that she had prepared. Later that day, he felt better and was able to resume his work but the following morning the same thing happened again. This time he asked Janet to fetch the doctor, which she initially refused to do, but, when he persisted, she gave way and sent for Dr Young. Writhing and vomiting, James told the doctor that he believed he was being poisoned. Young agreed but, before he could find an antidote, his patient expired.

As a result of the doctor's suspicions, Janet was arrested, and, when she protested that she had never bought any poison, Young reminded her that, the previous year, she had asked him for arsenic to kill vermin, but he had refused to supply it because he did not trust her. When a second doctor also refused to give her arsenic, she asked two women – Margaret Davison and Helen Aitkin – to buy both arsenic and laudanum on her behalf. A doctor supplied Margaret Davison with laudanum but refused to give her arsenic; but Dr Young himself had sold Helen Aitkin the poison believing that she needed it to deal with an infestation of rats.

Helen Aitkin gave the arsenic to Janet M'Lellan; and the following week, she asked her to obtain another sachet, explaining that a lodger had accidentally kicked over the saucer in which she had placed the contents of the first. As Dr Young's shop was closed, Helen bought the second sachet from a chemist.

At her trial, several witnesses gave evidence about the M'Lellans' unhappy marriage, which, they said, had become more fraught after the birth of the twins. Janet angrily denied their allegations, insisting that the children were her husband's and that Helen Aitkin was lying since she had never touched any kind of poison.

Her defence counsel, Mr Patton, set about destroying Helen Aitkin's credibility by pointing out that, since she lived an immoral life and had two illegitimate children, no reliance could be placed on her testimony. More significantly, he also produced a number of witnesses who testified that James had previously been suicidal.

The jury deliberated for under an hour before returning the verdict of not proven; and, as Janet M'Lellan walked free from the court, the case was largely unreported. In medical circles, though, it gave rise to discussions about the ease with which arsenic could be purchased, leading the *London Medical Gazette* to conclude that:

> "Had this woman been debarred access to poison, she might have murdered her husband by other ways but then we doubt whether, with clear proof of the cause of death, she would have so easily escaped."[28]

The case also raised questions in legal circles about the so-called 'bastard verdict' of not proven. The general consensus of opinion was that Janet was guilty of murder, but the jurors were so reluctant to see a woman hanged that, in spite of the evidence, they had chosen the easy option.

The debate changed nothing and, a decade later, in a far more celebrated case, another alleged murderess walked from the court a free woman.

The daughter of a wealthy Scottish architect, Madeleine Smith, like Christina Gilmour, began life with every material advantage. Attractive and intelligent, she was educated at a private school in London until, at the age of eighteen, she returned to the family home in an affluent area of Glasgow. Two years later, in April 1855, a mutual friend introduced her to Pierre Emile L'Angelier, a clerk in the warehouse of Huggins & Co., a Glaswegian brewery.

Madeleine and Pierre felt an immediate mutual attraction but, knowing Mr Smith would not approve of a match between his daughter and a man of such lowly station, they began meeting in secret. When her father discovered that they were exchanging intimate letters, he ordered her to put an end to their affair. Madeleine initially obeyed and avoided meeting Pierre but, within a short time, they resumed their passionate liaison with even greater intensity.

As Madeleine's bedroom was situated in the basement with direct access to the street, she was able to allow Pierre to enter unseen, once her parents were asleep. In their thrilling, secret fantasy world, they convinced themselves that they were married.

"Our intimacy has not been criminal," Madeleine wrote to her lover, "as I am your wife before God. You are my very dear little husband."[29]

Within twelve months, though, the excitement of their clandestine meetings began to wane as Madeleine realised that there could be no future with the lowly clerk. When a more appropriate suitor, of whom her parents approved, appeared, she accepted his proposal, intending to end the affair with Pierre. The wealthy merchant, William Minnoch, could offer her the comforts to which she had long been accustomed, and so, when the engagement was announced in January 1857, she wrote to her 'dear little husband', asking for the return of all her letters.

Pierre was devastated. He had always believed that one day he and Madeleine would marry, and, when he read of her engagement, he was so horrified that he not only refused to return the letters but also threatened to show them to her father and her fiancé. Frantic with fear, Madeleine pleaded with him not to ruin her reputation and her chance of future happiness, but Pierre responded by repeating his threat with greater vehemence.

Seeing that pleading would serve no purpose, Madeleine adopted a different approach, telling Pierre that there was no truth in the rumours of her betrothal to Minnoch; and that she only wanted to be with her dear little husband. To effect a reconciliation, she invited him to meet her on 19th February, which gave her plenty of time to purchase a packet of arsenic.

The morning after their rendezvous, Pierre's landlady found him writhing in agony and summoned a doctor, who treated him for 'a bilious derangement'. Within a couple of days, he had made a full recovery, but afterwards his symptoms recurred at frequent intervals. On 9th March, he told a friend that he had been seriously ill on two separate occasions after taking coffee and chocolate with Madeleine.

"It is a perfect fascination my attachment to that girl;" he said, "if she were to poison me, I would forgive her."[30]

Unbeknown to Pierre, Madeleine and Minnoch had been busily making plans for their wedding and, when the arrangements were completed, Madeleine purchased another sachet of arsenic.

On the evening of 22nd March, Pierre left home, telling his landlady that he had an appointment. Several hours later, she was awoken when he staggered into the house retching and clasping his arms across his stomach. She sent word to a doctor, who recommended laudanum and a mustard poultice but, by the early morning, the landlady was convinced that her lodger was dying.

The doctor returned and assured the anxious woman that there was no need to worry but, when he had left, Pierre murmured that the doctor was mistaken. He asked the landlady to draw the curtains so that he could rest, and, when she looked in on him soon afterwards, she found him dead.

His funeral took place two days later but his employers were so disconcerted by the sudden death of a healthy young man that they requested a post-mortem. As his body was exhumed, the police made discreet inquiries into his final days, and learned from his friends that he had spoken of some incriminating letters from a young lady, Madeleine Smith. When arsenic was found in his remains, Madeleine was arrested.

The press had a field day with the scandalous story of a seemingly respectable young woman and her not so respectable meetings with her secret lover. Readers lapped up the details with such relish that, when the trial opened on 30th June, the public gallery was crowded with spectators who had come armed with fruits and sandwiches, anticipating a lengthy hearing.

Unabashed at being the centre of attention, as Madeleine walked calmly into the dock, 'her step was as buoyant and her eyes as bright as if she were entering a box at the opera.'[31] Carrying a little lavender bag and a variety of smelling-salts, she took comfort from the knowledge that her father had employed the most skilled barrister who would ensure that the jury believed her plea of not guilty.

She had not anticipated the strength of the prosecution's case, presented by the Lord Advocate, James Montcrieff, who was able to demonstrate that she had the motive, means and opportunity for murder. Although no arsenic was found in her possession at the time of her arrest, witnesses swore that she had purchased the substance on three separate occasions; and, when her letters to Pierre were read aloud, the spectators were left in no doubt about her lack of moral character.

John Inglis, for the defence countered Montcrieff's arguments by showing that Madeleine had purchased arsenic for cosmetic purposes; and he used her letters to Pierre to suggest that the jilted lover was so distressed by her decision to end their affair that he had become suicidal. When his work colleagues were called to give evidence, one apprentice described how Pierre had seized a knife as though intending to kill himself, and another claimed he said he would jump off a bridge and drown himself in the river. Even his employer was forced to admit that Pierre had been thoroughly dejected:

> "He said he was truly miserable, and that he wished he was out of the world, or words to that effect. He was in a very melancholy state after this. He was gloomy and moody, and never spoke to anyone.'[32]

More pertinently, Inglis argued that there was no direct evidence to link Madeleine to the crime. No one had seen her administer poison to Pierre and, in spite of his landlady's evidence that he had gone out on the evening of his death, there were no witnesses to confirm that he had gone to meet Madeleine. Moreover, the post-mortem revealed such a large quantity of arsenic in his stomach that, according to the surgeon, it would have been impossible for anyone to ingest so much without knowing what he was doing.

In spite of this, the judge used his summing up to dismiss the idea of suicide, but he was equally quick to remind the jury to reach a verdict based solely on the law and the facts that had been set before them. In the event, they returned a verdict of not proven, and Madeleine was released.

By then, all hope of marrying Minnoch had faded, as he had broken off the engagement as soon as he heard about her affair with Pierre. Soon after the trial, though, Mr Smith offered a doctor named Tudor Hora a dowry of £20,000 to marry Madeleine and take her away to Australia.

Ironically, perhaps, Hora established a pharmacy in Perth, where, at his insistence, Madeleine lived incognito, spending her time playing the piano and always veiling her face when appearing in public. Nonetheless, her identity was eventually discovered and, when Hora heard himself described as the husband of a murderess, he sold his shop and the couple moved to Melbourne.

Accounts of what happened next vary, as some claim that, soon after their arrival in Melbourne, Madeleine left Hora and returned to England where she married George Wardle, with whom she had two children. Others describe this story as a myth, and insist that Madeleine remained childless. In any case, she was not with Wardle when, at the age of seventy, she married William Sheehy in the United States. In 1927, she died and was buried as Madeleine Sheehy in Mount Hope Cemetery in Manhattan.

Whether or not she poisoned her lover, the verdict saved her from the noose but her reputation was completely destroyed, and the rest of her life was ruined by her youthful indiscretions.

# Chapter 6 – The Angel in the House

Beyond a raised eyebrow or a frown of disapproval, few middle-class Victorians were shocked by reports of murders among the lower orders. From behind the façades of their respectable homes, the comfortably-off seldom came into contact with a world that was as alien to them as theirs was to the poor. In his 1845 novel *Sybil,* the future Prime Minister, Benjamin Disraeli, wrote that England comprised:

> "...two nations; between whom there is no intercourse and no sympathy; who are as ignorant of each other's habits, thoughts, and feelings, as if they were dwellers in different zones, or inhabitants of different planets; who are formed by a different breeding, are fed by a different food, are ordered by different manners, and are not governed by the same laws."[33]

Working women were an entirely different species to their counterparts in the middle and upper classes. While the former were engaged in heavy manual labour, the latter cultivated an image of frailty, protecting their pallid complexions from the sun, tight-lacing themselves into unhealthy shapes, and employing an army of maids to carry out any strenuous duties. The sole purpose of a middle-class woman was to serve as a docile wife and devoted mother, becoming in the words of the poet, Coventry Patmore, the 'angel in the house' who lived to make a comfortable home for her husband. She was expected to anticipate his needs, never thinking of – or even possessing – any passions of her own, as she should be devoid of sexual desires beyond what was required of her by her husband.

Consequently, while the middle-class were not shocked by the immorality of the poor, they were, as the case of Florence Maybrick showed, as horrified that an 'angel of the house' could commit adultery as that she could commit murder. Women who transgressed the moral code destroyed their own reputation and that of their family; and yet, at the same time, they were so irresistibly fascinating that, when a scandal broke, crowds flocked to courtrooms to catch every titillating detail.

For this reason, there were long queues for the public gallery when, in 1876, Florence Bravo, an attractive and independently wealthy woman, stood in the dock charged with the murder of her second husband.

Twelve years earlier, at the age of nineteen, Florence had married a wealthy but feckless Grenadier Guard, Alexander Ricardo, whom she persuaded to abandon his military career so that they could spend more time together. Deprived of his duties and the companionship of his comrades, Ricardo relieved his aimless existence with alcohol and the company of other women. When his drunkenness and womanising became too much to bear, Florence fled to Malvern where an eminent doctor, James Gully, had established a fashionable hydrotherapy clinic.

The unhappily-married Gully recognised in Florence a kindred spirit and, despite a forty-year age difference, he abused his position to begin an affair with his patient. When rumours of their liaison spread, Florence was shunned by society; and her horrified parents virtually disowned her, refusing to assist her financially so that she would be forced to return to her husband.

Fortunately for Florence, in 1871, Ricardo drank himself to death, leaving her a vast fortune with which she purchased an imposing house, The Priory, in Balham. Among several other servants, she employed a forty-three-year-old companion, Jane Cox, who encouraged her affair with Gully and accompanied the couple on several continental holidays.

After one such trip, when Florence reputedly returned home pregnant, Gully performed an abortion under the guise of removing a tumour. From then onwards, she became increasingly dejected, longing for acceptance and a reconciliation with her parents. Gully, realised that she could only regain her respectability by remarrying, and, when a rising barrister, Charles Bravo, proposed to her, he agreed to end their relationship so that she and Bravo could start a new life together.

Florence genuinely intended to make her second marriage a success and, shortly before the wedding in December 1875, she told her fiancé about her relationship with Gully. In response, Bravo admitted that he, too, had had a longstanding affair and had fathered a child by his mistress. Now, though, he said, they could begin anew, knowing that their marriage was grounded in honesty.

In reality, this was far from the case. Bravo had told a friend that he had no interest in Florence but only wanted access to her money; and, within days of the wedding, she realised that her second marriage would be more disastrous than the first. Bravo bullied and taunted her; dismissed some of her servants; complained about how much she drank; and ordered her to curb her extravagant spending. In the bedroom, he forced her to participate in 'unnatural practices', and, even after she had suffered two miscarriages in four months, he continued to demand his conjugal rights, with or without her consent.

Florence's plight was far from unique as rape within marriage was not seen as a crime; and a man had the right to imprison his wife to force her to yield to his sexual advances. As the law failed to protect them, many women dealt with over-amorous husbands by creating or buying concoctions, designed to quell a man's libido. It is possible that, with the help of Jane Cox, Florence obtained such a potion from Gully, and surreptitiously added it to Bravo's wine.

Alternatively, it is equally possible that Bravo was adding small amounts of poison to the Marsala that Florence drank so copiously. This would explain the regular bouts of illness that she suffered throughout her married life with Bravo.

One afternoon in April 1876, while Bravo was out riding, his horse threw him and dragged him some distance along the ground. He staggered back to The Priory, aching and exhausted, and that evening he ate a substantial meal washed down with a couple of glasses of Burgundy. Mrs Cox and Florence sat with him drinking sherry and Marsala until nine o'clock when Florence retired to her bedroom. Mrs Cox helped her into her nightclothes before returning downstairs to fetch more wine; and, a little while later, when a maid brought warm water, she, too, was asked to bring yet more Marsala.

On her way downstairs, the maid passed an angry-looking Charles Bravo, and she assumed that he was put out because he objected to the amount that his wife was drinking. He continued silently up the stairs and, after briefly calling into Florence's dressing room, he went to his own adjoining bedroom, closing the door behind him.

When Florence's ablutions were completed, the maid helped her into bed, and Mrs Cox sat on a chair beside her. As the maid walked back along the landing, Bravo suddenly charged from his room, desperately calling for Florence to bring him warm water. Not a little surprised that neither Florence nor Mrs Cox responded, the maid returned to the bedroom to tell them what was happening. Florence, who had imbibed vast quantities of wine, was already fast asleep, but Mrs Cox put down her knitting and calmly walked to Bravo's room, where he was vomiting out of the window.

She sent the maid for a specific doctor, who lived some distance away, before returning to Florence's room to explain the commotion. Not only was Florence genuinely concerned about her husband, but she was also astonished by Mrs Cox' choice of physician, and ordered that word be sent to one who lived far nearer to The Priory.

The doctor whom Florence had summoned arrived shortly afterwards and found Charles in a far worse state than he had anticipated. He lifted him onto his bed and tried to give him warm water and brandy, while awaiting the arrival of Mrs Cox' physician for a second opinion. By the time that the second doctor arrived, Bravo was vomiting blood; and Mrs Cox claimed that he had confessed to 'taking something.' When questioned about this, Bravo insisted that he had only taken a little laudanum to ease a toothache.

At a loss as to what to do, the doctors sent for a specialist, George Johnson, from King's College Hospital, to whom Bravo repeated that he had taken nothing but laudanum. For three days, his agonies continued while other doctors came and went and, although none could diagnose the cause of his illness, all agreed that he appeared to be on good terms with his wife, and that he never expressed the suspicion that he had been poisoned.

The moment that Charles Bravo died on 21st April 1876, the doctors examined every vessel in the room for traces of poison, but found nothing. It would have been more helpful, they concurred, if specimens of his excreta had been kept from the start of his illness, but all that remained was what he had vomited out of the window. This was scraped up and sent for analysis, which revealed traces of antimony, as did the deceased's organs during a post-mortem.

Although used less frequently than arsenic, antimony was taken as an anti-inflammatory treatment for rheumatism; and as a laxative, in the form of 'everlasting pills' which were swallowed whole and, having passed undigested through the gut, were excreted and washed for use by another patient! More commonly, it was used in veterinary prescriptions and, as it is relatively harmless to horses, it could be found in most stables as an equine skin treatment.

There was no evidence that antimony had ever been prescribed for anyone at The Priory, and so, while the inquest concluded that Bravo had died as a result of poisoning, there was no means of knowing how or by whom it had been administered or whether his death was due to an accident, suicide or murder.

Bravo's friends and family were most put out by this unsatisfactory verdict and demanded a second, more thorough inquest. In preparation, every detail of Florence's background, including her affair with Gully, was examined, and, when the second inquest opened three months later, women were barred from the hearing for fear that they would be shocked or corrupted. The popular press, however, produced such explicit reports of the relationship between Florence and her married lover that, whether or not she had killed her husband, her reputation and that of Dr Gully were ruined.

Ultimately, the inquest concluded that Bravo had not committed suicide but there was insufficient evidence to name the person who had administered the poison. Florence walked free but, as a result of the scandal, she was forced to sell The Priory and move out of London. She settled in Southsea, where she drank herself to death, dying only two years later at the age of twenty-eight.

Was Florence Bravo guilty of murder, or had she accidentally killed her husband by lacing his water jug with antimony to suppress his libido? Were her regular bouts of illness proof that Charles had been slowly poisoning her to gain full possession of her fortune; and had he accidentally taken the concoction that he had prepared for her? What of Mrs Cox? It was she who destroyed much of the evidence by ordering the servants to clear away Charles' vomit; and she, who told the doctors that he had spoken of suicide.

Moreover, a few days before Charles became ill, she had met Dr Gully, who could have provided her with poison[m].

Exactly a decade later, and less than five miles from Balham, a second perplexing case created another sensation, not least because of the unusual details of the central characters' marriage.

Reputedly the daughter of a wealthy Englishman, Adelaide Blanche de la Tremoille was born in France but spent the greater part of her childhood in England. In April 1875, at the age of nineteen, through some bizarre arrangement, she married a prosperous grocer, thirty-year-old Edwin Bartlett, whom she had met only once before the wedding. That sole pre-nuptial meeting was certainly intriguing as, according to Adelaide, she and Edwin agreed that they would never consummate their marriage. Whatever reasons Edwin gave for this decision, it must have come as a relief to his youthful bride, since his rotten teeth made his breath smell foul, and he regularly suffered from worms and various intestinal ailments.

Immediately after the wedding, Edwin packed his wife off to a boarding school, where she remained for two years before completing her education at a Belgian convent. In 1878, she finally returned to her husband, and although she had very few friends and even fewer entertainments, she appeared perfectly happy to occupy herself with her dogs and her sewing.

All was well until Edwin's widowed father moved in with the couple, and took an instant dislike to his daughter-in-law. He accused her of having an affair with Edwin's younger brother, Fred, who, in the light of the allegation, hastily departed for America. Whether or not there was any truth in the accusation, Edwin was so angry with his father that, in the presence of a solicitor, he forced

[m] For a more detailed analysis of Mrs Cox' possible involvement, see *Death at the Priory* by James Ruddick (Atlantic Books 2002)

him to apologise and to make a legally-binding promise that he would never repeat such slander, before throwing him out of the house.

Strangely, in view of the pre-nuptial agreement, soon after Fred's departure, Adelaide discovered that she was pregnant. With Edwin's consent, she placed herself under the care of an unqualified midwife, Annie Walker, who was ill-equipped to deal with any perinatal complications. When Adelaide endured a protracted labour, Annie, aware of her own limitations, urged Edwin to call a doctor but he refused to do so, saying that he would 'rather not have any man interfering with her.'[34]

Eventually, Adelaide gave birth to a stillborn baby, which left her so distraught that she tearfully told the midwife that she would have no more children, before adding – for no apparent reason – that Edwin's will stated that she would never inherit his considerable savings if she remarried after his death.

For two years, life continued at the same slow pace, until the Bartletts moved to Merton near Wimbledon, where they met a young Wesleyan clergyman, Reverend George Dyson. Edwin was so impressed by Dyson's intellect and learning that he asked him to help Adelaide to further her education. From then onwards, Edwin's adulation of the clergyman knew no bounds as he went out of his way to bring Dyson and Adelaide together. Edwin asked him to take care of her while he was away on business, and he even encouraged them to kiss one another in his presence. When the Bartletts went on holiday, Edwin paid for Dyson to join them; and, having altered his will to remove the stipulation about re-marriage, he asked Dyson to promise to care for Adelaide in the event of his own death.

"Dear George," he wrote to him, "…Would that I could find words to express my thankfulness to you for the very loving letter you sent Adelaide today. It would have done anybody good to see her overflowing with joy as she read it whilst walking along the street, and afterwards, as she read it to me. I felt my heart going out to you. I long to tell you how proud I feel at the thought I should soon be able to clasp the hand of the man who from his heart could pen such noble thoughts. Who can help loving you?"[35]

Unsurprisingly, Adelaide soon fell in love with the younger man who, while not strikingly handsome, was a pleasant contrast to her husband with his halitosis, intestinal problems and odd ideas about marriage. The clergyman's conscience was troubled, though, by his growing attraction to a married woman and he felt duty-bound to confess the truth to Edwin. He remorsefully offered to end their friendship and to move to another town, but, to his surprise, Edwin insisted that there was no problem at all and urged him to stay.

This unconventional ménage continued until December 1885 when the normally diligent Edwin came home from work earlier than usual because he felt unwell. The next day, although he felt no better, he accompanied Adelaide and Dyson to a dog show, but that evening, he complained of severe pain in his gut, diarrhoea and rectal bleeding.

Adelaide sent for a doctor named Leach, who discovered a thin blue line around Edwin's gums – a typical indication of mercury poisoning. As mercury was used to treat syphilis, Leach discreetly asked Edwin if he were suffering from venereal disease, but Edwin denied it but admitted taking a pill containing mercury some days earlier. This was not usual at the time, as mercury was used to treat a variety of other ailments, including parasites, which suggests that Edwin had taken it to combat worms.

The doctor ordered complete bedrest and a gentle sedative, which soon relieved his physical symptoms, but did nothing to ease his growing restlessness and depression. When, a week later, he was still prostrate with insomnia and gastric pains, Leach concluded that that his rotten teeth were to blame, and asked a dentist to visit him. Over the next eight days, the dentist removed fourteen decaying stumps, the pain of which intensified Edwin's depression.

Leach visited every day and, as visitors came and went, they all agreed that the patient could not have had a better nurse than Adelaide. All day she waited on him, and at night she slept in a chair by his bed, showing no revulsion at his unattractive condition. Only Edwin's father found cause for complaint, when Adelaide, who had not forgiven his insult, only allowed him to visit on three occasions.

Mistrustful and angry, the senior Mr Bartlett declared that he would call his own doctor to give a second opinion, but Edwin replied that he would not see him, as he was sure that he was getting better thanks to Leach's treatment. Leach, unwilling to be embroiled in a family dispute, said that he had no objections to interventions from other doctors, to which Edwin replied that, although he would not see anyone whom his father sent, he would willingly be examined by a doctor chosen by Leach, 'for the protection of my wife.' When Leach asked him what he meant, Adelaide replied:

"Mr. Bartlett's friends will accuse me of poisoning him if he does not get out soon."[36]

The following day, Leach introduced Edwin to his colleague, Dr Dudley, who was convinced that his ailments were psychosomatic. He recommended that he should spend time outdoors to raise his spirits, and he privately told Leach that he was sure that Edwin would already have recovered if Adelaide were not so quick to wait upon him.

Christmas came and went and, when Edwin still showed no signs of improvement, Adelaide asked Dyson to obtain some chloroform to relieve his insomnia. Annie

Walker, she said, usually provided it for her, but, as the midwife was spending Christmas in America, she needed an alternative supply.

Chloroform had been used as an anaesthetic for almost forty years and had gained greater respectability when it was given to Queen Victoria to relieve the pain of childbirth. Nonetheless, medical supervision was required in its administration, as, if it were dispensed carelessly, it could cause fatal cardiac dysrhythmia. Consequently, Dyson hesitated and suggested that Adelaide should seek Leach's advice, but she replied that the doctor was unaware of her skill in its administration.

The next day, in spite of his reservations, Dyson purchased four bottles of chloroform from three separate chemists, and, having poured the contents into one larger vessel, he took it to the Bartletts' home but waited until a guest had left before handing it to Adelaide.

Meanwhile, Edwin continued to deteriorate as worms infested his gut, and his few remaining rotting teeth caused necrosis in his jaw. On New Year's Eve, after much persuasion, he managed to drag himself to the dentist's surgery, and, on returning home after more extractions, he ate a hearty meal.

Adelaide played the part of an adoring wife more devotedly than ever. Regardless of his rotting jaw, his cavernous gums, his worms and his hypochondria, she told the doctor that she wished that they were not married so that she could experience the joy of her wedding day once more! She made a point, too, of telling her landlady that Edwin often took a few drops of chloroform to help him to sleep.

In the early hours of New Year's Day 1886, the landlord was rudely awoken by a frantic hammering on his door and Adelaide begging him to come at once as she feared that her husband was dead. He followed her upstairs and, finding the body completely cold, he concluded that

Edwin must have been dead for at least a couple of hours. Adelaide hastily explained that she had nodded off to sleep and, when she awoke and saw how still he was, she had tried to revive him by pouring half a pint of brandy down his throat.

Leach was summoned and immediately noticed that a fire had been stoked in the grate, giving lie to Adelaide's claim that she had hurried at once to fetch the landlord. He noticed, too, that the odour of chloroform pervaded the room, and, fearing the worst, he ordered a post-mortem.

The initial examination the following afternoon failed to find the cause of death, but, when Edwin's stomach contents were analysed by Dr Stevenson, it was clear that he had died as a result of taking chloroform. As soon as Adelaide heard his report, she gave Dr Stevenson a full account of her marriage. Edwin, she said, had not only brought her and Dyson together but had actually declared that they belonged to one another. During his final illness, she continued, Edwin had a change of heart, and, after years of abstinence, he suddenly wished to exercise his conjugal rights. So urgent were his amorous advances that she could only deter him by sprinkling chloroform onto a handkerchief and waving it in his face until he fell asleep. On New Year's Eve, she confessed to Edwin that this was what she had been doing and as proof she showed him the bottle that she kept on the mantelpiece. In view of Dr Stevenson's report, she could only conclude that, after she had fallen asleep, Edwin had imbibed the chloroform of his own volition.

Old Mr Bartlett, meanwhile, was telling all and sundry that his son had been murdered, which so frightened Dyson that he turned on Adelaide, confessing that he had purchased the chloroform as he had been 'duped' by the 'wicked woman.'

On February 18th, the coroner's inquest returned a verdict of wilful murder against Adelaide Bartlett, and named Dyson as an accessory after the fact. Both were detained in custody pending their trial at the Old Bailey but, on the morning of hearing, the judge announced that the charge against Dyson had been dropped in return for his turning Queen's evidence.

In her favour, Adelaide obtained the services of a brilliant barrister, Sir Edward Clarke, who abandoned all his other clients and spent the days prior to the trial reading the case papers and studying medical books to discover the effects of chloroform.

"The week was to me one of very great strain," he wrote. "I made a point of being at my place in court every morning before the judge came in, so that when the fragile, pale little woman came up the prison stairs to take her place in the dock she should see in the crowded court at least one friendly face."[37]

The prosecution asserted that Adelaide had drugged Edwin by wafting chloroform in his face before pouring the remaining contents of the bottle down his throat when he was unconscious. Clarke, however, was able to dismiss this hypothesis by showing that, if that had been the case, some of the chloroform would have entered the wind-pipe and its effects would have been evident during the post-mortem.

Having cast doubt on the medical evidence, Clarke emphasised the possibility that Edwin had committed suicide. Although his teeth had caused him much pain, his doctors had concurred that his illnesses were largely psychosomatic, and that he had taken to his bed as a result of depression. Moreover, on the final evening of his life, Adelaide had told him that their marriage was over as he had given her to Dyson. When his spirits were at their lowest ebb after several sleepless nights, he saw the bottle of chloroform on the mantelpiece and swallowed its contents. Although the story seemed plausible, it did not account for the absence of burns in his mouth, throat and gullet.

Clarke then drew attention to Adelaide's behaviour when she saw that Edwin was dead. She summoned help and sent for a doctor, and she had encouraged Leach to press for a post-mortem.

In an impassioned speech that lasted for over six hours, the barrister employed all the rhetoric of a great orator, urging the jury to look kindly on the unfortunate and friendless woman whose life was now in their hands. So powerful was his monologue that, much to the judge's annoyance, when he had finished, the entire courtroom erupted into applause.

The judge presented a fair summing up of the case, during which he completely destroyed Dyson's reputation. The clergyman, he said, had taken advantage of Edwin's unbalanced state of mind to win Adelaide's affection and, therefore, his evidence should be discounted. The jury retired to consider the verdict, returning after an hour to ask what time the Bartlett household usually went to sleep. Having received a satisfactory reply, they retired again before retaking their seats in the courtroom. The clerk asked, 'Do you find Adelaide Bartlett guilty or not guilty of murder?'

"Although," the foreman replied, "we think there is the gravest suspicion attaching to the prisoner, we do not think there is sufficient evidence to show how or by whom the chloroform was administered."[38]

Had the case been heard in Scotland, this would have led to a verdict of not proven, but in England there were only two options: guilty or not guilty. The clerk, therefore, asked again, "Does this mean you find the prisoner not guilty?"

To which the foreman firmly replied, "Not guilty."

Clarke, in an uncharacteristic show of emotion, burst into tears while Adelaide fainted and had to be carried from the dock.

"No other verdict," reported the Times, "could be expected, but the Pimlico mystery is as much a mystery as ever...Whether on the theory of guilt or innocence, the whole story was marvellous!"[39]

Queen Victoria's surgeon-general, Sir James Paget, remarked that, once the trial was over and she had been acquitted, Adelaide should, in the interests of science, have explained how the chloroform came to be in Edwin's stomach.

In a case of many mysteries, there is one final puzzle: what happened to Adelaide Bartlett after the trial? She repaired at once to Brighton, from where she wrote to thank Clarke for his services, after which she disappears from historical records. It has been suggested that she and Dyson married and settled in America, but there are equally convincing claims that Dyson, wanting nothing more to do with her, emigrated to Australia.

# Chapter 7 – By Reason of Insanity

At the dawn of the nineteenth century, madness was seen as a domestic issue to be dealt with in private by members of the family. The wealthy locked away their afflicted relatives in remote rooms within their own homes, giving rise to the notion of the 'madwoman in the attic' so beloved by Gothic novelists. Alternatively, they could pay for care in a private madhouse, where conditions were often appalling as inmates were guarded by ill-educated and drunken minders.

Apart from a few pennies from the parish, the only provision for the poor was the London Bethlehem Hospital ('Bedlam'), designed to house the 'pauper insane.' Chained in cells, the inmates, who ranged from the mildly demented to the criminally insane, became a tourist attraction, as, for a fee, the public could gawp at them, in much the same way as they gawped at 'the bearded lady' or the 'freaks' on display at a fair.

It was only when the king[n] himself suffered periods of insanity that medical men and politicians decided that more provisions were required to deal with the problem of madness. In 1808, the County Asylums Act encouraged local councils to build new premises to contain 'pauper lunatics and imbeciles', but few counties responded to the suggestion, and almost forty years would pass before any real attempt was made to address the issue.

In 1845, Lord Shaftesbury chaired a Lunacy Commission, which led to a marked change in attitudes towards mental illness. For the first time, the afflicted were viewed as patients rather than prisoners, and, following the introduction of the new Lunacy Act, vast asylums were created to focus on healing rather than detention. Staffed by medical officers, they aimed to treat the patients with

---

[n] King George III – Queen Victoria's grandfather – is believed to have been suffering from porphyria.

consideration and kindness; and arranged meaningful work for them to aid their recovery. Complete with their own farms, fields, bakeries and pharmacies, they formed self-sufficient villages, wherein the 'mad' could find a safe haven – or asylum – in a pleasant location.°

Little by little, as the century progressed, old prejudices gave way to a new understanding so that, in 1884, one doctor was able to state that:

> "The public are learning that asylums are merely brain-hospitals, and that their inmates find in them a comfortable home and kindly and skilful care; hence there is no longer the senseless dislike to these institutions which formerly existed, and the relatives of patients thankfully accept their aid for afflicted friends."[40]

Since asylums were now recognised as hospitals rather than prisons, the medical staff were reluctant to house criminals among their patients. Consequently, a separate institution was required for the criminally insane, and, to that end, the Criminal Lunacy Act of 1860 led to the construction of Broadmoor, which opened in Berkshire in 1863.

The first female inmates of Broadmoor were transferred from the London Bethlehem Hospital and included Mary Ann Parr, who had smothered her illegitimate baby; and Sarah Allen, who had thrown her three children into the Thames. Their crimes were typical of the majority of Broadmoor's female inmates, most of whom were incarcerated for killing their own children.

One such woman was Sarah Dickinson, whose problems first surfaced in 1837, when, while working as a housemaid, she became so confused that her employer took her to her sister's house in the hope that a familiar face might bring her to her senses. After several days, she made

---

° As asylums were often reached by winding country lanes, they gave rise to the term 'going round the bend.'

a complete recovery and, at the time of her wedding soon afterwards, her friends described her as rational and cheerful.

Over the next two years, she gave birth to two children, George and Jane, to whom she was a devoted mother.

There was no recurrence of a mental illness until, while staying with her brother-in-law, she had a serious fall. From then onwards she was often gloomy or vacant; she frequently complained of pains in her head; and sometimes cried out that she feared she was losing her senses. To make matters worse, her husband, John, fell ill and was no longer able to work, which meant that she had the added stress of a dire financial situation. Her neighbours urged her to seek help from the Poor Law Guardians but, as she refused to do so, she and John often went without food so that they could give what little they had to their children.

On the evening of 10th January 1844, John returned home to find Sarah, George and Jane lying on the blood-soaked bed with their throats cut and a razor lying beside them. Reeling in shock, he ran to his neighbours, who discovered that Sarah was still breathing despite her horrific injuries. They sent for the police, who initially assumed that John was the culprit, but, when a surgeon skilfully stitched Sarah's severed windpipe, she gasped that she was responsible for the killings.

For the next few days, her life hung in the balance but, as she slowly began to recover, her doctors monitored her closely for any signs of insanity. They observed several episodes of 'aberrant behaviour', during which she appeared completely unaware of what she was doing. In her more lucid moments, she was utterly distraught about what she had done to her children.

By the beginning of March, she was well enough to stand trial at the Old Bailey, where she presented 'a most miserable appearance'. The medical witnesses for the defence testified that she was unaware of what she was doing at the time of the murders, and, despite the prosecution's attempts to show that she knew that murder was wrong, the jury returned a verdict of 'not guilty by reason of insanity', and she was taken to Broadmoor.

A year later, a similar and equally tragic case occurred when twenty-one-year-old Eliza Huntsman of Edmonton in London drowned her five-month-old baby in a fit of madness. For over twelve months, Eliza had shown signs of mental disturbance and often complained of severe pains in her head, which her doctor treated by shaving off all her hair. She was prone to sitting vacantly for hours before suddenly leaping up and becoming hyperactive and distraught.

Unlike Sarah Dickinson, Eliza had few financial worries, as she lived with a kindly aunt, who later testified that she always took good care of her baby. On the afternoon of 10th December 1845, her aunt's daughter was visiting when Eliza, who had been perfectly calm, suddenly flew into a panic crying, "My baby! My baby!"

It was soon established that the little girl was missing, but, as Eliza could not remember where she had left her, her cousin sought help from the police. An officer spotted a child's bonnet lying on a grassy bank and, for the next three hours, he and a colleague dredged the adjacent stream until they came upon the dead baby.

Eliza was arrested and, four days later, she appeared at the Old Bailey, where medical experts discussed several bizarre theories to explain her insanity. The most outlandish suggestion was based on the fact that she had hired a wet-nurse because, said the doctors, she was unable to express her milk, which had flowed inwards and affected her brain!

Whether or not the jury believed the preposterous hypothesis, Eliza was found not guilty and her case was dismissed.

A strikingly high number of women who pleaded not guilty of murder by reason of insanity could trace their problems back to a fall or a blow to the head, followed by chronic headaches. In 1883, for example, Sarah Ellen Procter's brother struck her for insulting their mother, and, as she ran away from him, her foot caught in her dress and she fell face-first onto a brick drain. The doctor who attended her found her concussed and in need of stitches; and, in the longer term, her behaviour changed and she constantly complained of severe pains in her head.

Two years after her fall, Sarah, while working as a nail-maker, was carrying a bag of nails on her head, when her friend, Charlotte Whale, hit her for some unknown reason, causing blood to flow from her ear. From then onwards, her paranoia became more extreme and her behaviour more erratic but, in spite of what had happened, she remained friends with Charlotte Whale, and incident with the nails soon appeared to be forgotten.

In 1888, Sarah and Charlotte travelled together from Staffordshire to London in the hope of finding work in a market garden. Arriving in the city, they stayed with Charlotte's friends, the Callows, in a house that was so overcrowded that the two women had to share a bed.

That evening, they appeared to be on very good terms but, early the following morning, Sarah seized a jug and repeatedly smashed it over Charlotte's head so violently that a part of the brain protruded through the gashes. When the police arrived, she calmly admitted that she had done it and that she would be hanged.

During her trial in the Old Bailey, her sister gave evidence that several members of their family were subject to fits, and their father had frequently been unable to work because he 'suffered in his head.' A doctor, who had examined the prisoner while she was in custody, opined that she had inherited a mild form of epilepsy but also had an inflammation of the membranes of the brain. Found not guilty by reason of insanity, Sarah was sentenced to be detained in an asylum 'at Her Majesty's pleasure.'

Emma Aston, likewise complained of feeling pressure on the top of her head immediately prior to murdering her two children to whom, until then, she had shown herself to be a kind and loving mother. Her situation was particularly tragic not only because of the deep remorse she felt for what she had done, but also because it is unlikely that she would have done it, were it not for the callousness of the father of her children.

In 1882, she had a well-paid job as a forewoman in a mantle factory when she became pregnant by another employee, a married man, Jack Morris. The child lived for only three months, and Emma returned to the factory, resuming her position until 1886, when she again became pregnant with Morris' baby. When a little boy, Bertie, was born, Morris paid for Emma's lodgings, and he continued to contribute to her upkeep until she gave birth to another of his sons, Frank, a year later.

By then, though, Emma was thirty-eight and no longer had the charm that had first attracted Morris to her. As he moved on to a younger mistress, he reduced the payments to Emma, forcing her to leave her lodgings and find rooms in a small terraced house in Upton Park. For the sake of appearances, she gave her name as 'Mrs Styles' and told her landlady that her husband was a commercial traveller, who worked away from home.

Within months, Morris, enraptured by his new lover, abandoned Emma altogether, leaving her with no income to care for the boys. Bills mounted; the rent was in arrears; and Emma was suffering from a liver complaint and neuralgia. On 20th February 1888, she felt pressure on her head and sudden compulsion to murder her children. She stabbed them both in the head with a knife and, having failed to kill them, placed a pillow over their faces until they died of suffocation.

During her trial at the Old Bailey, medical experts agreed that, although she appeared perfectly sane, at the time of the crime she was not responsible for her actions as, in those moments, she did not know that what she was doing was wrong. The stress of poverty, desperation, exhaustion and physical pain had made her behave irrationally; and, as soon as she came to her senses, she regretted what she had done.

She was found not guilty by reason of insanity, and as, by the time of her trial, she had completely regained her senses, the judge wrote to the Home Secretary, Henry Matthews, recommending that she should be immediately released. Matthews, however, ordered her to be detained in Broadmoor for six months so that doctors could examine her mental state more thoroughly. Free from the stresses of the outside world and the need to fend for herself, Emma settled so happily into the asylum that, when the six months was over, she was in no hurry to leave. Moreover, as some of the medics believed that she had killed the children while suffering from puerperal mania, it was deemed advisable to keep her incarcerated until she was beyond the age of childbearing[p].

By the time that she was released, at the age of forty-eight, she had become so institutionalised that she could not cope in the outside world. Within weeks, of her own volition, she returned to Broadmoor, where she remained for the rest of her life.

Once the initial crimes had been reported, the press paid little attention to the fates of Eliza Huntsman, Emma Aston and Sarah Dickinson, but, in 1852, a similar case attracted far more media attention due to the prisoner's

[p] See Chapter 9

direct connection to Queen Victoria and King Leopold I of the Belgians.

In 1816, Queen Victoria's uncle, Prince Leopold of Saxe-Coburg, married Princess Charlotte of Wales – the daughter and heir of King George IV. As a wedding gift, the couple was given Claremont House in Esher, where they lived until Princess Charlotte's untimely death in childbirth in 1818. Among their staff was a groundsman, George Brough; and his wife, a kitchen maid, Mary Ann, whose father also served as a coachman to Prince Leopold.

In 1831, the widowed Prince Leopold was chosen as King of the Belgians but, although he moved to Brussels, he retained his English property and his staff. The Broughs continued to work for him, living in a comfortable cottage on the Claremont estate where they raised their numerous children. When, in 1841, George Brough heard that Queen Victoria was seeking a wet-nurse for her second child, 'Bertie', the Prince of Wales, he recommended Mary Ann, who, he said, was 'quiet and temperate in her habits'.

Mary Ann began well, even attending the baby prince's christening, but, by the time that Bertie was eight months old, the Queen and Prince Albert found her so 'morose, ill-tempered and stupid' that they dismissed her from their service. For the next eleven years she lived quietly with her husband, giving birth to six more children, while George continued to tend the oriental ponds for Claremont House's most recent occupants: the family of King Leopold's father-in-law, the deposed King Louis Philippe of France.

A week after the birth of her youngest child in 1852, forty-year-old Mary Ann suffered a stroke, which left her with a permanent speech impairment and temporary hemiplegia. From them onwards, she suffered from severe headaches, nose bleeds and migraine-like symptoms, some of which her doctor, Mr Izod, believed were psychosomatic. He advised her to avoid all excitement and, for the next two years, he regularly visited to provide her with a variety of medications.

In spite of her ailments, her husband began to suspect that she was having an affair and, in the summer of 1854, he became so suspicious that he hired a detective to follow her. The detective reported that Mary Ann had met a man in a tavern, which later led the press to imply, without any justification, that she was working in a brothel. On hearing of her clandestine meeting, George was so angry that he left her and threatened to return to take the children with him.

A few days later, two workmen were passing Mary Ann's cottage at six o'clock in the morning when they spotted a blood-soaked pillow hanging out of an upstairs window. Fearing that there had been an accident, they hammered on the door and, receiving no reply, brought a ladder to climb up to the bedroom. On the bed they found two children whose throats had been cut, and Mary Ann lying beside them in a similar condition. Moving into adjacent rooms, they found four more children, all of whom had been killed by the same method. Mr Izod was summoned and confirmed that all six children were dead but, as Mary Ann was still breathing, he sent for a surgeon, Mr Mott, who stitched her windpipe, saving her life. Far from being grateful, Mary Ann gasped that she wished she had succeeded in killing herself.

Although she was immediately arrested, her trial was postponed pending her recovery, and, in the meantime, her children were buried in a sombre ceremony in Esher. George Brough was so distraught that he had to be carried from the graveyard, while, from her sickbed, Mary Ann reiterated that she wished that she, too, were dead.

"It is truly enough to make all the children of the village afraid of their mothers," remarked King Louis Philippe's son, the Prince of Joinville; and Queen Victoria could only shake her head in horror at the 'depraved life' that Bertie's former wet nurse must have lived.

When she was well enough to be interviewed by the police, Mary Ann gave no excuse for her actions apart from explaining that she had felt a great black cloud around her. All the children, she said, had been asleep when she killed them, except for the youngest, who was wide awake and consequently harder to kill. She went on to explain that, when she had finished her horrific task:

"I lay down and did myself. I can't tell you what occurred for some time after that till I seemed weak, and found myself on the floor. That nasty great black cloud was gone then. Then I was thirsty, and I got the water-bottle, and drank. I fell in a sitting position. I sat a little while and got up and saw the children, and it all came to me again. I wished to call, but could not speak. I did not know what to do. I went to the window, and put something out to attract attention."[41]

Her neighbours were aghast that so devoted a mother could turn on her children, and, during her trial in Guilford, they attested that she had always treated them well.

"I have frequently seen the prisoner with her children," said the workman who discovered the bodies, "and she always appeared to be very good and kind to them."

The psychiatrist, Dr Forbes Winslow, interviewed her prior to the trial, and gave evidence that, although she appeared perfectly rational during their conversation, her nose bleeds and temporary paralysis were evidence of 'a congested brain.'

"Cases of temporary insanity resulting in a desire to commit murder or suicide are very common," he said rather chillingly. "I have known many instances where the patient has made an attack upon some near relative with whom he had previously been on the most affectionate terms, and it frequently occurs with mothers and children. In such cases the patient suddenly suffers under a strong homicidal impulse which he cannot control; and it has happened to me to hear a patient bitterly lament being under the influence of such an impulse. The impulse is generally stronger in proportion as the parties are more nearly and dearly connected, and to the previous affection existing between them."[42]

Mary Ann was found not guilty by reason of insanity, and ordered to be detained in Bedlam.

One unanticipated drawback of the new asylums was the doctors' eagerness to declare their patients healed. Basing their diagnoses on the behaviour of the patients within the confines of the institution, they overlooked the possibility of a recurrence of their problems when faced with the pressures of the outside world.

In September 1889, for example, Elizabeth White was admitted to a private asylum, suffering from paranoia and delusions of extreme poverty. After only ten weeks, the overseers decided to release her despite the reservations of the senior medical officer, who advised her husband to ensure that she was constantly guarded. During her absence, her husband had employed Mary Deeley to care for their children and, in view of the doctor's recommendation, he asked her to stay and watch over his wife when she returned home.

For the first three days, despite being rather apathetic, Elizabeth calmly helped Mary around the house but, on the fourth day, her behaviour suddenly changed. While Mary was busy dealing with the baby, Elizabeth took the three elder children into an adjoining room, locked the door behind her, and started to strangle them. Hearing the commotion, Mary desperately tried to break in but, being unable to do so, she ran out and called to two stablemen for assistance. The men managed to force the door and found two children already dead while Elizabeth was trying to strangle a third. They restrained her until a policeman arrived, to whom Elizabeth confessed that she had intended to kill them all as there was no left to care for them. On being arrested, she asked if the eldest child would survive, and, when she was told that he probably would, she replied sadly that she wished he would die since he had nothing to live for.

Elizabeth was taken to Holloway Prison pending her trial, which resulted in a verdict of not guilty by reason of insanity. The judge ordered that she should be detained indefinitely as he had no doubt that she would kill again if she were ever released.

A month later, Eleanor Jacobs followed her into the dock at the Old Bailey, charged with the murder of her illegitimate daughter, four-year-old Emily. She, too, had previously spent time in an asylum, to which her mother had committed her due to her erratic behaviour during her pregnancy. Following her release, she initially seemed to have made a full recovery, but she soon relapsed, often bursting into tears, destroying her clothes, cutting off her hair, and occasionally threatening to kill her mother. Nonetheless, she doted on her daughter and no one in the family had any concerns for the little girl's safety.

One morning in January 1890, Eleanor and Emily were lying in the bed that they shared, when the child said that she was hungry and asked for a piece of bread. Eleanor calmly took her down to the kitchen and attempted to strangle her before seizing a poker and beating her to death.

Almost instantly, she came to her senses and ran back upstairs to tell her mother what she had done. Her mother hurried out to find a policeman and, when Inspector Bunting arrived at the house, Eleanor calmly said that

Emily was better off now than if she were still living. Unsurprisingly, she was found not guilty by reason of insanity and ordered to be detained indefinitely.

# Chapter 8 – I Have Done Murder

As life in a psychiatric hospital with the possibility of eventual release was infinitely preferable to death by hanging, barristers often urged their clients to plead insanity as a means of avoiding a capital sentence when the evidence was clearly stacked against them. Juries were then expected to decide if a prisoner were faking madness – an almost impossible task for unlearned jurymen when even the sharpest legal minds in the country struggled to find a means to determine whether a murderer was 'mad' or merely 'wicked.'

An early attempt to resolve the issue was made in 1843 when Daniel M'Naghten, while suffering from paranoid delusions, shot dead Robert Peel's Private Secretary, Edmund Drummond, whom he had mistaken for the Prime Minister. A panel of judges used the case to create the M'Naghtan Rules, which stated that the jury must presume the sanity of a prisoner unless the defence counsel proved otherwise; but a prisoner was guilty only if he knew what he was doing and that what he was doing was wrong.

Although the guidelines set out reasonable principles, they were of little use to juries who were presented with conflicting evidence from medical experts with opposing opinions. In many cases, their decisions led to criticism and controversy and never more so than in the case of Celestina Sommer

A daughter of a respectable silversmith, William Christmas, Celestina – 'a pale-faced, fair-haired woman of spare form'[43] – was raised in a comfortable home in Islington, where she received a good education and enjoyed the companionship of her seven siblings. Her life began to unravel when, at the age of eighteen, she brought shame on the family by giving birth to an illegitimate daughter, whom she also named Celestina.

To avoid further scandal, the child was placed in the care of a paid minder, with whom she lived quite happily for almost a decade. In the meantime, Celestina married a hot-tempered Prussian engraver, Charles Sommer, who responded to her erratic behaviour by beating her.

Eighteen months after the wedding, she suddenly decided to reclaim her daughter, whom she had not seen for almost ten years. On the night of 16th February 1856, she collected the little girl from the minder, took her back to her Islington home, led her into the coal cellar and slit her throat. Charles Sommer was out that evening but the sixteen-year-old maid, Rachel Munt, heard the child's desperate cries. Rather than going to help, Rachel was so terrified that she stayed in bed, hiding under the covers.

In the morning, when she went into the cellar, she found the little girl's body but still did nothing until her sister happened to visit. When Rachel told her what she had seen, the sister ran to a police station and returned to the house with Inspector Hutton and Constable Townsend. The policemen searched the cellar and, having found the body, prepared to arrest Celestina and her husband. Charles, however, produced a solid alibi and so Celestina alone was taken into custody.

When her trial opened at the Old Bailey in April 1856, her barrister, William Ballantine, argued that she had not been in her right mind at the time of the murder. His argument was strengthened by the evidence of the police officers, who attested that, while in custody, she talked to herself incessantly about which actors should play the leading roles in Shakespeare's *Richard III* and *Hamlet*. When questioned, she confessed to murdering little Celestina, whom she claimed was her late brother's child. Asked why she had killed her, she frankly replied, "I did it because I did not know what else to do."[q]

---

[q] Although it was never discussed at the trial, there is no record of who actually fathered Celestina Christmas, which begs the question: was she

The jury came to the conclusion that Celestina's behaviour was a charade and she was faking madness to avoid a capital sentence. They, therefore, returned a guilty verdict but no sooner had Mr Justice Creswell sentenced her to death than petitions poured in to the Home Secretary, who commuted the sentence to life imprisonment.

The public and several prominent psychiatrists were outraged by this outcome, arguing that premeditation proved that Celestina knew what she was doing. Even opponents of capital punishment shared their indignation, pointing out that other women were hanged for less heinous crimes, whereas Celestina was spared the gallows although 'few instances of more unrelenting cruelty have been recorded.'

She was taken first to Millbank Prison, where she appeared to be perfectly sane and compliant, although she never expressed any remorse for the crime. On one occasion, a chaplain asked her if she regretted killing her daughter, to which she replied mechanically, 'Oh! of course, I am very sorry! I say a great many prayers a day, you know. Very sorry, very sorry, indeed!' before rapidly changing the subject.

After eight months, she was transferred to Brixton, where her mental and physical health declined so rapidly that much of her time was spent in the infirmary. During periods of recreation, she did not associate with the other prisoners but walked purposefully around the yard, talking to herself, much to the amusement of her fellow inmates.

At first, the prison authorities suspected that she was faking insanity when she blurted out incoherent statements or sang at the top of her voice during communal prayers. Soon, though, her behaviour became so outlandish that she was removed to the Fisherton House Lunatic Asylum.

---

the result of an incestuous relationship between Celestina Sommer and her brother?

"During her stay at Brixton Prison," wrote the prison matron, "she evinced great concern at no one calling to see her, and used to fret a great deal at this neglect, or seeming neglect, of attention on the part of those whom she thought dear to her. This was her only trouble whilst her mind retained any semblance of coherent ideas; but a time came when the true and the false – the real and the unreal – blended themselves inextricably together."[44]

She remained at Fisherton House for only five months until her death at the age of thirty-one in 1859. By the end of her life she truly was insane, but whether that were so at the time of the murder remains a mystery.

Coincidentally, sixteen years after the death of Celestina Christmas, Islington was the setting for another tragic case in which a mother slit the throat of her little girl. Lydia Venables attacked her daughter, Eliza, while she was lying in bed, and, when a lodger, hearing the commotion, burst into the room, Lydia calmly said that the child was now happier as there was no future for her on earth.

The tragedy of the situation became clear during the subsequent investigation. Three years earlier, Lydia had been widowed but had recently moved in with a cabman, Alfred Chatterton, whose wife had abandoned him and their eight-year-old daughter. By his own admission, Chatterton had a fiery temper, and, on the evening of the murder, he and Lydia had a violent argument, during which he struck her and told her to leave, taking Eliza with her.

At her trial in the Old Bailey, the distraught Chatterton blamed himself for what had happened, believing that his temper had driven Lydia to murder. As a result of his testimony, her defence attempted to reduce the charge to manslaughter but the judge would not hear of it, insisting that there was no excuse for such an appalling crime.

Lydia was found guilty and sentenced to hang but within a week her sentence was commuted to five years imprisonment. In fact, after serving only three years, she was granted an unconditional release.

It was not uncommon, as in Lydia's case, for a judge to intervene when a barrister attempted to present his client as insane. When, for example, Mary Gallop's defence pointed out that madness ran in her family, the judge remarked that far too many defendants were claiming insanity with no justification. In this case, he was probably correct to dismiss the suggestion that Mary Gallop was *non compos mentis,* but her barrister might have saved her had he pressed for the lesser charge of manslaughter on the grounds of extreme provocation.

In 1837, the year of Queen Victoria's accession, the Grand Junction Railway Company opened a station and locomotive works in the township of Monks Coppenhall in Cheshire. Over the next decade, as 'railway mania' gripped the country, thousands of workers migrated to the area and, out of a once sleepy hamlet, emerged the prosperous town of Crewe.

Among those thousands of workers was a Liverpudlian joiner, Richard Gallop, who arrived in Monks Coppenhall in the spring of 1844 with his wife; their daughter, Mary; and the daughter of Mrs Gallop's first marriage. Richard alone had made the decision to move from Liverpool, much to the chagrin of nineteen-year-old Mary, who had been forced to leave a suitor, Duval, of whom her father did not approve. Her unpredictable mother was equally distressed by the upheaval but, as with every other aspect of her life, her husband made the rules and she obeyed without question.

No one could deny that Richard was an obstinate bully, whose behaviour might have contributed to his wife's mental decline. Almost twenty years earlier, there were rumours that she was insane while pregnant with Mary; and when, two months after arriving in Crewe, she slit her own throat with a razor, many believed that Richard's mistreatment had driven her to suicide.

Deeply affected by her mother's death, Mary did not sleep for two months but wandered around in a daze. Eventually, though, she managed to regain her equilibrium, and devoted herself to teaching at the local Methodist Sunday School, as well as waiting on her father and a lodger named Frazer, who had moved into their home.

Far from showing remorse about his wife's suicide, Richard simply transferred his bullying to Mary. If his meals were not to his liking, he threatened to beat her; and he forbade her from going anywhere without his permission. Life became so unbearable that she considered going into domestic service solely to escape his aggression but, in October 1844, she chanced upon a railway company notice that brought a glimmer of light into her otherwise dreary existence.

The company was advertising cheap tickets to Liverpool; and Mary's heart lifted at the prospect of seeing her old friends and Duval again. When, though, she mentioned the idea to Richard he adamantly refused to allow her to go.

Mary's resentment was still festering when she saw a rat in the house and mentioned to her half-sister that they ought to buy some poison. When her half-sister casually replied that she had read of a woman who used rat poison to kill her husband, an idea began to take root in Mary's mind. By chance, at that time, Richard had developed a bowel complaint which Mary believed had similar symptoms to poisoning. On 1st November, she bought two pennies' worth of arsenic, telling the chemist that her father had sent her to buy it to kill a rat.

That afternoon, she baked four cakes: one each for herself and her sister; one for Frazer; and one for her father, which she laced with the poison. To her great disappointment, Richard was not hungry, but, when she and the others ate their cakes, they all became ill and did not recover until the following morning.

Realising that she must have accidentally mixed some of the arsenic with the flour, Mary returned to the chemist and bought another sachet. This time, she placed the whole amount in the arrowroot that her father took for his bowel complaint, and the effect was almost instantaneous. He complained of griping in his gut, followed by a series of bouts of vomiting and diarrhoea, and, as he continued to deteriorate overnight, a doctor diagnosed cholera.

By morning, Richard Gallop was dead, and, as was the custom, a constable arrived to find out what had happened. Had Mary remained quiet, no one would have questioned the doctor's diagnosis, but she panicked and mentioned that she had recently bought arsenic. The constable made a cursory search and, finding two loaves and the cake that Richard had not eaten, he sent them with Richard's arrowroot, to Liverpool for analysis.

When Richard's post-mortem showed that he had been poisoned with arsenic, Mary's half-sister described how they had all been ill after eating the cakes that Mary had baked. Mary was arrested and, having been charged with murder, she was detained pending the Chester Assizes.

During her trial, her barrister, Mr Trafford, initially tried to persuade the jury that Richard had taken the arsenic by mistake, but, sensing that this argument was making little impression, he switched tack and suggested that, if Mary had administered the poison, she had done so during an episode of insanity. Her mother's suicide, he said, showed that insanity ran in the family; and Mary's behaviour after her death showed that she, too, was afflicted by mental illness. In view of the judge's comments, however, the jury took only five minutes to find her guilty, and, when the foreman added a plea for mercy, the judge indignantly replied that there were no grounds for such a plea, and, donning his black cap, he sentenced Mary to death.

Many prominent figures, including the Bishop of Chester and future Archbishop of Canterbury, petitioned for a reprieve, pointing out Mary's previous good character and the work she had done at the Methodist Sunday School. Their efforts were in vain.

When the officials came to lead her to the gallows on a cold December morning, Mary was so overcome with fear that she had to be carried, and was allowed to remain seated throughout the procedure.

Few people criticised the judge's refusal to accept Mary Gallop's plea of insanity, but when, in 1899, the judge at the trial of Mary Ann Ansell declared that she was sane and described her as a cold-blooded killer, his remarks provoked outrage across the country and led to a fiery debate in Parliament.

Eighteen-year-old Mary Ann worked as a housemaid in London, where her exhausting duties were brightened by the prospect of her forthcoming wedding, which was planned for Easter 1899. Unfortunately, in the early autumn of 1898, her fiancé realised that his income was insufficient to support a wife and family, and so he and Mary Ann agreed to postpone the wedding for a couple of months in in the hope that, by then, they would be in a better financial situation.

A few weeks later, Mary Ann took out a life insurance policy on her twenty-six-year-old sister, Caroline, who, for the past four years, had been confined in the Leavesden Imbeciles Asylum in Watford. If Caroline died after six months, Mary Ann would receive the princely sum of twenty-two pounds and ten shillings, which, she later claimed, she intended to use for a decent funeral.

Throughout the early months of 1899, Mary Ann made regular purchases of phosphorus paste to poison the rats, which she claimed had infested her employer's kitchen. As its name suggests, the paste contained yellow phosphorus which, if ingested, causes gastro-intestinal irritation followed by multiple organ failure. The employer, however, later stated that she was unaware of the infestation; and that the maid must have paid for the poison out of her own money.

Caroline, meanwhile, began to receive a number of food parcels supposedly from her cousin; as well as a series of letters, one of which wrongly informed that both her parents had died. On 9th March – six months after Mary Ann had taken out the life insurance policy – she received a cake, which she shared with four other patients, all of whom were struck down with stomach pains and vomiting. A few days later, as her friends recovered, Caroline died. The coroner ordered a post-mortem and, when it was determined that she had died of phosphorus poisoning, Mary Ann was arrested as she attempted to claim on the life insurance policy.

At her trial in Hertford, her barrister, William Clarke Hall, argued that Mary Ann had been on good terms with her sister and there was no proof that she had sent the poisonous packages. Convinced that she would be released, Mary Ann remained perfectly calm throughout the proceedings, and even when she was found guilty and the judge sentenced her to death for her 'revolting and cold-blooded crime', she smiled contentedly as though she were completely unaware of what was happening.

A number of observers were deeply disturbed by the conduct of the trial, not least because Clarke Hall failed to mention the extent of insanity in the Ansell family. Two of Mary Ann's sisters had been certified as 'imbeciles' and two of her aunts had died in a lunatic asylum. Moreover, when the psychiatrist, Lyttleton Forbes Winslow, investigated her background, he learned from her teachers, employers and the prison chaplain that 'this unfortunate creature is mentally deficient and childish, and never seemed to have the least idea of moral responsibility.'[45]

Her poor parents, overcome with grief, could hardly believe their misfortune. Mary Ann, they insisted, was a good girl but was 'always queer', sometimes refusing to talk to them for no apparent reason. When the *Daily Mail* took up the story, the Home Secretary, Matthew White Ridley, was bombarded with petitions for a reprieve; and even the foreman of the jury stated that, if he and his fellow jurors had been given more information about the familial insanity, they would never have returned a guilty verdict.

A hundred Members of Parliament were so uneasy about the verdict that they presented a paper to the Home Secretary:

> "We, the undersigned members of the House of Commons, respectfully suggest to the Right Honourable Sir Matthew White Ridley the desirability of postponing the execution of Mary Ansell for at least a week, to enable further inquiry to be made into her mental condition, seeing that a great diversity of opinion exists on the question."[46]

White Ridley, unmoved by the petitions, replied that he had considered the evidence and saw no reason to overturn the judge's decision. Mary Ann was hanged by James Billington in Hertford Prison on 19th July 1899.

# Chapter 9 – Concealment of Birth

One evening in the early spring of 1844, Thomas Gardener was walking his dog along the banks of the Regents Canal when he heard a vague moaning, and, turning, saw a woman floating in the water, carrying a bundle under her arm. Seizing a boat-hook, he managed to pull her to safety, and, unwrapping the bundle, found it contained a small boy.

Although the child was not breathing, Gardener picked him up and ran to the nearest inn, where he called for a doctor. The little boy was immersed in a warm bath in the hope that it would revive him but the doctor soon confirmed that he was dead.

The woman, meanwhile, had been taken to the outhouse of the inn where, shivering and distraught, she gave her name as Mary Furley. She asked about her little boy, George, and, when told that he had died, she became frantic but did not protest when she was arrested for his murder.

In the days that followed, she recounted the tragic story of what had brought her to the brink of suicide and murder. Her troubles began when her husband abandoned her and their two young children, leaving them so destitute that they were forced to seek refuge in the Whitechapel Workhouse. Contrary to expectations, the overseers treated them well, and Mary soon felt sufficiently confident to take the children from the workhouse to make her own way in the world.

Sadly, it was not long before she was again forced to seek refuge, this time in the Bethnal Green Workhouse, where, according to Mary, conditions were inferior to those in Whitechapel. Although she was well-treated, four-year-old George was so undernourished that he developed a skin infection, resembling impetigo. When sores erupted on his face and head, his hair was shaved off on four separate occasions, and, the fourth time, the barber was drunk and cut into his scalp. Mary was so distressed that she decided to take him from the workhouse, and was given a small sum of money from the Poor Law Guardians to support her and George until she found work as a seamstress.

She began stitching shirts, but, as the pittance she earned was barely enough to live on, she decided to use what little money she had to purchase some ribbon to make fancy hats instead. On her way to the shop, she claimed, her purse was lost or stolen and, despairing at the prospect of being forced to return yet again to the workhouse, she threw herself into the canal, holding George in her arms.

During her trial at the Old Bailey, other workhouse inmates denied that George had been undernourished, and attested that their own children had thrived in Bethnal Green. Moreover, the surgeon who performed the post-mortem, gave evidence that, at the time of his death, George had been in good health and showed no signs of malnutrition.

As prisoners were not permitted to give evidence, Mary's barrister read out a statement that she had prepared. This, too, contradicted her earlier account of what had happened, as she now claimed that she had never intended to kill herself or the child, but had slipped on a plank and fallen with him into the canal.

In spite of the discrepancies, Mary's tragic tale earned so much public sympathy that it was widely believed that she would be charged with a lesser offence or acquitted. The judge, Mr Justice Maule, however, showed no compassion whatsoever and, on passing the death sentence, he warned her not to hold out any expectation of mercy.

She was taken to Newgate Prison to await execution but well-wishers continued to urge her not to lose heart. Vast numbers of people petitioned the Home Secretary, Sir James Graham, and the general expectation was that he would grant a reprieve. This encouragement served only to increase Mary's horror when, on 4th May 1844, the sheriff, Mr Musgrove, accompanied by the prison governor and the chaplain, entered her cell to inform her that she would be executed two days later. Mary burst into tears and for the next twenty-four hours she was left in a state of abject terror until suddenly, the following afternoon, the sheriff returned to tell her that Sir James Graham had commuted her sentence to seven years transportation to the colonies[r].

Far from rejoicing at the outcome, the press unanimously condemned the Home Secretary not only for putting Mary through twenty-four hours of mental agony but also for failing to grant her a complete reprieve. Her case had highlighted the desperate straits in which many single mothers found themselves, and went some way to altering the perception of women who, in desperation, murdered their children.

Infanticide – the killing of a child under one year old – was far and away the most common form of murder committed by women in the nineteenth century. In just four years between 1852 and 1856, over six hundred mothers were charged with having suffocated, poisoned, starved, drowned or even decapitated their babies. This, though, was but the tip of the iceberg as many more such crimes went undetected. In fact, it was so easy to dispose of a deceased baby that Londoners were reluctant to touch any packages left in the street for fear that they would contain tiny corpses.

Surprisingly, in an age which is often viewed as harsh and judgemental, the judiciary showed remarkable compassion and leniency towards women who committed infanticide. Henry Hawkins, a renowned High Court Judge, described, with great sympathy, a case which came before him bearing many similarities to that of Mary Furley. A

---

[r] See Chapter 19

young woman, intending to kill herself and her one-week-old baby, had waded into a river but, although the baby drowned, she was fished out by a passing boatman. At her trial for murder, the judge took pity on her and, although he was bound by law to pass the death sentence, he planned in advance the report he would send to the Home Secretary to secure her reprieve.

"I was about to pronounce sentence in accordance with the law, which it was not possible for me to avoid, however much my mind was inclined to do so," he later recorded, "when the pompous old High Sheriff, all importance and dignity, said:

'My lord, are you not going to put on the black cap?'

'No,' I answered, 'I am not. I do not intend the poor creature to be hanged, and I am not going to frighten her to death.'

Addressing her by name, I said: 'Don't pay any attention to what I am going to read. No harm will be done to you. I am sure you did not know in your great trouble and sorrow what you were doing, and I will take care to represent your case so that nothing will harm you in the way of punishment.'

I then mumbled over the words of the sentence of death, taking care that the poor creature did not hear them, much, no doubt, to the chagrin of the High Sheriff and to the lowering of his high office and dignity."[47]

Rather than suggesting that she was insane, which would necessitate her being confined in an asylum, the judge reported to the Home Secretary that the prisoner had suffered a mental aberration at the time of the baby's drowning, and consequently he secured an acquittal.

For the most part, the public would have appreciated the judge's efforts, as women and girls who committed infanticide were often viewed more with compassion than with condemnation.

> "There is no crime," a member of the Royal College of Surgeons reported bitterly, "that meets with so much sympathy, often of the most ill-judged kind; and an almost partisan feeling has frequently been evinced, not only by the legal, but even by the medical profession."[48]

This sympathy sprang from the assumption that the killers acted through desperation or in the throes of 'puerperal mania' – an extreme mood disorder occurring after childbirth. The condition, which was first diagnosed in the eighteenth century, is seen nowadays as extremely rare but, in the Victorian era, it was believed to affect one in every eight-hundred women. The symptoms varied widely, ranging from complete apathy to mania or violent rages; and, as doctors struggled to explain the cause, some argued that it was triggered by excessive kindness from relatives, or even the excitement of reading too much after childbirth. Several self-righteousness medics were quick to point out that the condition was most prevalent among unmarried mothers:

> "In their case the pangs of labour are assuaged by no moral consolation; the present is full of anguish, and the future is lighted by no ray of hope. Can we wonder that these poor creatures, predisposed to disease by the combination of every moral as well as physical cause which could depress their vital powers, indifferent to life, nay, even, as I have but too often heard them, wishing for death – should under such circumstances, be peculiarly liable to puerperal mania."[49]

Patients suffering from the condition were usually confined in asylums, where they were denied visitors to prevent over-excitement. The length of their stay depended on the extent of their mania but there was, according to one psychiatrist, 'a small class among these who may, perhaps, with a degree of safety be liberated after a sufficient lapse of time – namely, those who have committed infanticide under the influence of puerperal mania – after the period of childbearing has passed.'[50]

Puerperal mania was not mentioned during the trial of Sarah Featherstone, although she was clearly suffering from a mental disorder when she murdered her baby boy. A well-educated and intelligent girl, she had fallen in love with a young man who promised to marry her but, when she became pregnant, he abandoned her.

After the baby was born, Sarah turned to prayer in desperation, and, opening her Bible in the hope of finding guidance, she chanced upon a line from the Book of Deuteronomy: 'A bastard shall not be admitted into the congregation.'

Taking this as a sign, she tearfully carried her baby to a pond and, having fastened stones into his clothes, placed him in the water. As the little bundle floated away and started sinking, she suddenly came to her senses and frantically fished around with a stick in the vain hope of saving him.

Arrested and charged with murder, she appeared at the Chester Assizes where she was found guilty with a recommendation to mercy. The law demanded that she should hang but the judge, Baron Martin, who was 'always very brief in his sentences and never attempted to harrow a prisoner's feelings'[51], felt such compassion for her that he refused to sign the death warrant until he had sent the details of the case to the Home Secretary, Lord Palmerston.

At the last moment, Palmerston commuted the sentence to life imprisonment, and Sarah was taken to Brixton Gaol, where she accepted her fate so patiently that she endeared herself to the staff and the other prisoners.

"I have a remembrance of her suffering twice from pleurisy," wrote the prison matron, "and of her taking all the ills that flesh is heir to, with a gentleness and patience characteristic of her under every circumstance. She was a constant reader of her Bible; on her sick-bed or in her cell she seemed to derive much comfort from its perusal, and much resignation to her own hard fate. She was…patient, uncomplaining, and reverent, deserving of every merciful consideration; and I am disposed to think that, when free pardons are bestowed on any of the women gathered together in these shadowy folds, Sarah Featherstone will not be entirely forgotten."[52]

Thousands of young women of the era could have sympathised with Sarah's plight, knowing the dire consequences of having a child out of wedlock. If an unmarried girl became pregnant, she would inevitably lose her employment and, in many cases, find herself cast out from her family. With her reputation in ruins and her prospects bleak, her only recourse was the workhouse, where she would be expected to undertake heavy manual duties almost up to the moment that she went into labour. Once the baby was born, she was allowed to stay in the infirmary for two weeks before being forced to decide whether she wished to remain in the workhouse, where she would be separated from her baby, or leave, taking the infant with her.

"They could stay and be paupers," wrote the Manchester Poor Law Guardian, Emmeline Pankhurst, "or they could leave – leave with a two-week old baby in their arms, without hope, without a home, without money, without anywhere to go..."[53]

Many, who opted for the latter course, struggled to survive until, out of desperation, they were forced to return to the workhouse or they killed their babies.

"Often," wrote Dr Forbes Winslow, "…child murders, so frequently recorded, are perpetrated with…coolness. The parent claims the prescriptive right of doing what she conceives the best for her offspring, and, in this instance, it seems best to her perverted judgment that she should protect herself from scandal, and remove her child from misery and want simply by the act of taking its life. She brings herself to the conclusion that what would be wilful murder in another is in her own case nothing but a laudable course of prudence and decision."[54]

This was the conclusion drawn by Emily Church when, on becoming pregnant, she was dismissed from her post as a servant and was forced to seek refuge in the workhouse. After fifteen months, she decided to leave, taking her baby daughter to the home of her Aunt Isabelle, in the hope that her aunt would look after the child so that she could work in a local jute factory.

Unfortunately, relations between the two women soon deteriorated as Emily complained that her aunt was not taking good care of the baby; and Aunt Isabelle accused her niece of not paying her way. After a few months, Emily left for Barking, where she placed the child in the care of a minder so that she could earn a living picking peas. The minder soon proved too expensive, and Emily had no option but to take the child back to her aunt to plead with her to resume her care. When Aunt Isabelle agreed on condition that Emily sent regular payments for her daughter's upkeep, Emily promised to do so and returned to Barking.

Three weeks passed and, as Aunt Isabelle received no payment, she took the child to Barking, intending to leave her with her mother. Emily was not at home and so she left the little girl in the care of her landlady, Mrs Brittain, and, when Emily returned in the evening, she was surprised to find her daughter waiting for her. She played with her for an hour before telling Mrs Brittain that she was going out in search of a new childminder.

Later that evening, she returned home having failed in her endeavour, and, the following afternoon, she told the landlady that she was taking the child to Stratford where she hoped she could find better paid work than pea-picking. Four days later, Emily returned alone to her lodgings, telling Mrs Brittain that she had left her daughter in the care of a minder in nearby Rainham.

The next day, two labourers found the naked body of a female child tied up in a bundle of rags, floating in a brook. A post-mortem revealed that she had died from a blow to the head and had been placed in the water after death. The police learned that Emily had been seen in the area but, when she was questioned, she denied ever having had any children. A policeman asked her to accompany him to the inquest in a nearby inn, and, on the way, she admitted that she had a daughter whom she had left with a woman in Rainham. As she was unable to give the minder's name or address, she was charged with murder.

At her trial at the Old Bailey, the evidence against her was so conclusive that the jury took only several minutes to find her guilty, but they added a recommendation of mercy on the grounds of her extreme poverty. Malnourished, terrified and exhausted, she fainted in the dock when the judge pronounced the death sentence, prompting several men in the public gallery to burst into tears. Fortunately for her, the Home Secretary was also moved by her story and, within a week, he had commuted her sentence to life imprisonment.

A high proportion of infanticides were committed by domestic servants, many of whom had been seduced by their employers. A life in service often began at the age of thirteen, and naïve girls far from home were easy prey for older men who occupied positions of authority. Lady Constance Lytton, a daughter of a Viceroy of India and a lady-in-waiting to Queen Victoria, met one such woman who was imprisoned in Holloway Gaol.

"She was a servant, and had been seduced by her master. She, of course, was dismissed from his service. When the child was born, he had at first contributed to its support, but after a while had ceased to do so and disappeared, leaving no address. She had taken the greatest pride in bringing up her child, a boy, to whom she was devoted...As time went on the struggle to maintain herself and her child was considerable. She made a friend, a man of her own class, who knew her history, respected her for her good motherhood and promised to marry her as soon as a sufficiently good job came his way...The work failed, marriage prospects paled, her friend deserted her and she found herself faced with the prospect which she now understood only too well, of disabled health, unemployment, disgrace, and a second child to maintain unaided. She kept on at her employment in a laundry until the very hour of her premature confinement. Then worn out in body and spirit, and quite alone at the moment of her trouble, she had in her distraction and misery strangled her baby. She went on with her work at the laundry. It was the father of her child who gave her up to the police; according to one rendering, he did so because she was so ill he thought it the only way to secure for her 'a rest.'"[55]

More often than not in such cases, prisoners were not charged with murder but rather with the lesser crime of concealment of birth. Even this, though, carried a custodial sentence and, following their release from prison, it was very difficult for offenders to find employment.

The prospect of losing a job and falling into destitution was so terrifying for some young women that they concealed their pregnancies, and abandoned or murdered their babies as soon as they were born. Margaret Marshall, for example, hid her pregnancy from her employer; gave birth in a privy; and stuffed the baby down the sewage pipe where it bled to death, soaked in excrement. Others in similar circumstances dumped their infants on street corners, up chimneys and down drains.

In early 1867, Eliza Forrest suspected that her new housemaid, Letitia Dordy, was pregnant – a fact that the maid vehemently denied. Eliza's suspicions increased when, on the morning of February 22nd, she walked into the kitchen and found Letitia cleaning up pools of blood. Determined to discover what was happening, Eliza sent the maid on an errand and, during her absence, made a thorough search of the house. On finding a dead baby in Letitia's bedroom, she called to a policeman, who arrested the maid as soon as she returned.

Letitia claimed that the child was stillborn but, when a post-mortem revealed that the cause of death was suffocation, she was charged with both concealment of birth and murder. The Liverpool jury found her guilty but her abject and exhausted appearance aroused so much sympathy that her capital sentence was reduced to life imprisonment.

A similar case occurred a decade later when Mary Mahoney, an eighteen-year-old servant, working at Ffynnonwen Farm near Cardiff, gave birth to a little girl in the early hours of the morning. She hid the baby in a water closet but, when she began to cry, Mary panicked and struck the poor child on the head with a coal pick. The crying stopped; the baby was dead; and Mary wrapped the little body in an apron, which she stuffed behind some sacks at the back of a barn, intending to dispose of it more thoroughly later.

By then, though, it was morning and, when a labourer walked into the barn, he spotted the bundle and saw a tiny hand sticking out from the apron. Maintaining his composure, he locked the bundle in a granary store and repaired to the police station to tell Constable Hill what he had seen. Hill accompanied him back to the farm and, having examined the bundle, began questioning the servants. Mary at once admitted that the baby was hers but initially claimed that it had been stillborn. Only when Hill had taken her into custody did she break down and make a full confession.

While awaiting trial at the Swansea Assizes, the horror of what she had done and the prospect of being hanged so terrified the wretched girl that the wardresses feared that she had lost her mind. Raised as a Roman Catholic, she believed that she had committed a mortal sin, and the thought of eternal damnation literally frightened her out of her wits.

Fortunately, she was visited by the kindly prison chaplain, who calmed her fears and helped her find consolation in the hope of redemption. Nonetheless, when she appeared in court, she was greeted with such hostility from the public gallery that, for a while, it appeared that she would collapse into total insanity. The judge took pity on her and, when the jury found her guilty, he told her that, although he was required by law to pass the death sentence, he would write to the Home Secretary, Richard Cross, with a recommendation for mercy.

Screaming in terror, Mary was led away.

The judge was not the only one to contact the Home Secretary. As soon as the sentence was pronounced, large numbers of local people, church-goers and women's groups launched a series of petitions, which persuaded Cross to commute the sentence to life imprisonment. Mary, though, filled with remorse, still struggled to come to terms with what she had done and, during her imprisonment, her mental state deteriorated.

Surprisingly, her story had something of a happy ending. After eight years in prison, she was released to the care of a prisoners' support group, who arranged for her to be placed in a comfortable care home, where she quietly lived out the rest of her days in relative peace.

The majority of women who committed infanticide did so out of fear of destitution, but for others the prospect of losing a respectable reputation was an equally powerful motive. Sarah Lipman, a thirty-year-old widow, owned a second-hand clothes shop, from which she earned a sufficient living to employ a maid. When, though, her customers whispered that she was pregnant, she realised that her indiscretion could damage her business and her good name.

As soon as she went into labour, she shut herself into a room at the back of the shop and, having delivered the baby, she began to cut it up and throw it into the fire. Before her grisly task was completed, the maid walked in and was aghast to see blood all over the floor and a little hand in the flames.

Sarah, pleading with her to say nothing, offered her a sovereign to clean up the room, but the maid was so horrified that she ran from shop and told a passing policeman what she had seen. The officer accompanied her back to the shop, where he found Sarah sitting, exhausted and soaked in blood; and the baby's head still warm in the fireplace. A surgeon was summoned, who arranged for Sarah to be taken to the workhouse infirmary, where she remained until her trial two weeks later.

It was symptomatic of an undercurrent of antisemitism that, when the press reported the story, they played into the age-old calumny that portrayed the Jews as baby-killers. Fortunately, although the headlines screamed of a 'horrible murder of a child by a Jewess', the judiciary took a more balanced view, and, when the surgeon stated that the baby was premature and would have died anyway, the murder charge was reduced to concealment of birth.

# Chapter 10 – Inconvenient Children

A strange contradiction characterised the Victorian attitude towards children: while art and literature portrayed them as cherubic innocents in need of protection, their real-life counterparts were seen as wild creatures in need of being tamed. Platitudes about the necessity of discipline and obedience hung on the walls of workhouses and homes where overseers and fathers adopted the maxim 'spare the rod and spoil the child' as a basis for good child-rearing.

Attitudes to the death of a child were similarly contradictory. When infant mortality rates were so high that one in five children died before their fifth birthday, the death of a baby was often met with resignation rather than grief. Queen Victoria, a devoted grandmother, remarked on the death of one of her many grandchildren that the loss of a child could not be compared to the loss of a husband. At the same time, grown men cried in the street when they read of the death of Dickens' Little Nell; and children's tombstones were the most ornate monuments in the graveyard.

Respectable people who never gave a thought to the dangers facing juvenile factory workers, were outraged when they read of the murder of a child; and the sympathy felt for desperate young mothers who committed infanticide did not extend to those who disposed of their children simply because they had become an inconvenience.

When her lover fled the country to avoid his responsibilities, Sarah Baker struggled to care for their baby boy. Destitute and dejected, she was unable to bond with the child, being, in her own words, 'reduced to such a depressed state of body and mind' that she pulled a blanket over his face and threw him into a coal pit.

"I was obliged to throw the little beggar over," she later confessed, "it made such an awful row."[56]

In view of her extreme poverty and depressed state of mind, her sentence was commuted to life imprisonment. This came as no hardship to her after a lifetime of hunger and insecurity, and she settled so cheerfully into the Millbank Prison that her diligence and good-humour impressed the governor. The matron, though, was appalled by the heartlessness with which she spoke of the murder.

> "I am inclined to think," she wrote, "that a great deal of public sympathy was wasted on this woman, and that for the crime itself, and its consequences, Baker felt little remorse. There was a hardness, even a callousness in her manner of alluding to the crime, that showed the heart had not been wrung much by the guilty act which had deprived her child of life."[57]

There was even less sympathy for women who murdered their children because they stood in the way of their plans to build a new life with a new lover. Ann Wycherley, for example, inspired nothing but disgust when she callously stoned her little daughter to death.

In all fairness, twenty-eight-year-old Ann had lived a dreary, unhappy life, and was described at the time as 'simple-minded' and 'close to idiotcy'. On a bitterly cold day in December 1837, she walked out of the Market Drayton Workhouse with her two illegitimate children in tow. The elder child, three-year-old Ann, was the daughter of a former partner; the younger, one-year-old Jane, was the daughter of her current lover, Charles Gilbert.

As Gilbert had made it plain that he would not care for another's man's child, Ann dragged the children three miles through the snow from the workhouse to a remote chalk pit, where she pelted the older girl with stones and, tossing her into a pool in the pit, left her for dead.

Eight days passed before two farmers found the three-year-old's battered body, which they carried to the nearest house and sent for the constable. The governor of the workhouse identified the child, but, when Ann was arrested, she initially denied all knowledge of the murder, stating that her daughter was safe and well in nearby Fair Oak. The constable took her into custody and, the following morning, when he took her to see the body, she admitted that she had pushed little Ann into the chalk pit but insisted that Gilbert had forced her to do it, and he was the one threw the stones that killed her.

Gilbert was also arrested but, as there was no evidence against him, he was soon released, leading Ann to stand alone in the dock at the Stafford Lent Assizes in March 1838, with no friends to support her, and no legal team to present a defence. When the judge passed the death sentence, she claimed to be pregnant, but, as this was soon disproved, she was taken to Stafford Gaol to await execution.

The prison chaplain, Richard Buckridge, presented a petition for clemency on the grounds that she was simple-minded and had been coerced by Gilbert into committing the crime. He drew attention, too, to the unfairness of a trial, in which so ignorant a woman had no legal counsel to speak for her. The Home Secretary and future Prime Minister, Lord John Russell, saw no reason for granting a reprieve; and on 5th May, Ann calmly walked to the scaffold, resigned to her fate.

In view of the chaplain's arguments, Russell's failure to commute Ann Wycherley's sentence appears incomprehensible, particularly as it is clear that she had not received a fair trial; but the pressure upon Home Secretaries, holding the power over life and death in their hands, was immense and their decisions almost invariably met with criticism.

> "The duty of the Home Secretary in advising the Queen in the exercise of her prerogative of mercy was beset with difficulty," wrote a contemporary of Sir George Grey, who served in that office three times between 1846 and 1866. "It was impossible

for Sir George Grey to escape criticism, however he acted; but his legal training stood him in good stead. He neglected no pains to make up his mind, and he arrived at his conclusion under a deep sense of responsibility. But when he had done his best he adhered resolutely to his opinion, while those who dissented from him had no ground to complain of want of attention to their opinions."[58]

Inevitably, mistakes were made, and the unpredictability of Home Secretaries' decisions can be clearly illustrated by comparing the outcome of two similar cases with entirely different outcomes.

The first case involved Elizabeth Harris who, after giving birth in a workhouse in 1856, decided to take the new baby, Tommy, to live with his father in Portsmouth. The only problem was that she had two elder daughters, Ellen and Agnes, who was lame. She doubted that Tommy's father would be willing to provide for the girls; and, what was more, she did not have enough money to buy them train tickets to Portsmouth. Before departing, she told her niece that she was going to find somewhere for Ellen and Agnes to stay; and she left the house with the girls in tow. Twenty minutes later, she returned home alone.

That evening, when a labourer on his way home from work, found the children's bodies floating in the Grand Union Canal, witnesses told the police that Elizabeth and her daughters had been seen on the bridge and, soon afterwards, she had been seen on her own. She was found in an inn and initially denied that she was Elizabeth Harris but, when her sister was brought to identify her, she agreed to go to the morgue to see the bodies. Displaying no emotion, she kissed the children and confirmed that they were her daughters, adding that they had no father to protect them.

'Prostrated in terror and grief' throughout her trial, she looked 'more dead than alive' when Mr Justice Compton pronounced the death sentence.

The second case took place in June 1878, when Selina Wadge left the workhouse with her two children: six-year-old John, and two-year-old Harry, who was severely disabled. Unable to cope on her own, she took the boys to her mother's home in Cornwall, where she soon became friendly with a soldier, James Westwood.

On 22nd June, she and her sons set off to meet Westwood in Launceston, hitching a lift on a farmer's wagon to the outskirts of the town. Soon afterwards, Selina was seen with only the elder boy, and, when acquaintances asked what had happened to Harry, she gave several different answers: he was staying in Launceston; he was with her mother; he had sadly passed away.

Westwood failed to appear for the rendezvous, and, by the following evening, Selina was back in the workhouse with little John. When the matron asked where Harry was, she replied that he had died and been buried in the local churchyard. Neither the matron nor the workhouse superintendent believed her story, and, in the course of their inquiries, they learned that the boy had disappeared somewhere near Launceston. When they questioned Selina further, she said that Westwood had thrown him into a pit and he had drowned.

A couple of hours later, she again changed her story, admitting that she had killed Harry because Westwood had promised to marry her but refused to take care of her disabled son. When the allegation was put to Westwood, he was utterly astounded, insisting that he had only met Selina on two occasions, and had never even contemplated, let alone mentioned, marriage.

During her trial, workhouse officials and neighbours attested that Selina had previously been of good character and had always taken care of her children.

Nonetheless, the jury found her guilty of murder, adding a strong recommendation for mercy.

In both Selina's case and that of Elizabeth Harris, petitions were sent to the Home Secretary and prayers were said for a reprieve on the grounds of extreme poverty and ignorance. Richard Cross, the Home Secretary at the time of Selina's trial, dismissed the petitions, and, at eight o'clock in the morning on Monday 15th August 1878, she walked 'with a firm step' to the scaffold to be hanged 'in the utmost secrecy.'

Elizabeth Harris was more fortunate as the Home Secretary, Sir George Grey, commuted the sentence to life imprisonment.

In Millbank Gaol, she quietly carried out her duties, regularly reading the Bible and cheerfully accepting her fate. At no time, though, did she show any remorse for killing two innocent children, and, according to the matron:

> "She was a woman who showed no little real gratitude for any kindness, which she returned with that irritable, jealous affection common to many prisoners besides herself. This proneness to jealousy was Elizabeth Harris's greatest fault. It annoyed her to hear a single word of kindness addressed ta her companions in the ward, and she would take it into her head to maintain a rigid silence for many days after a kind word spoken to another prisoner. She never betrayed passion, or even suffered herself to be led into an insolent demeanour, or give a sharp answer during her brooding fits; but contented herself with dark looks at the woman who had received the envied word or smile, and responded to her matron in brief monosyllable."[59]

These two different outcomes demonstrate the arbitrary nature of obtaining a reprieve, depending entirely on the judgement of the Home Secretary. Both women were poor and both had spent many months in the workhouse but, in spite of having killed two children, Elizabeth Harris escaped execution; while Selina Wadge, a previously good and caring mother, was hanged for the murder of one son.

Some cases, like that of Louisa Masset, were far less controversial, as even the most lenient Home Secretary would have had little inclination to commute the sentence of a woman who could use neither poverty nor ignorance as an excuse for the cold-blooded murder of a three-year-old child.

In April 1896, French-born Louisa arrived in England with her baby son, Manfred, whom she placed in the care of the appropriately-named Miss Gentle in Tottenham at a cost of one-pound-and-seventeen-shillings a week. Attractive and well-educated, Louisa made a reasonable living, working as a governess by day, and giving piano lessons in the evenings. In spite of her busy schedule, she eventually found time to embark on a romantic relationship with nineteen-year-old Eudore Lucas – a French bank clerk, almost twenty-years her junior.

In 1899, enthralled by her new lover, Louisa began to view her illegitimate child as an encumbrance, the cost of whose upkeep would be better spent elsewhere. In October, therefore, she wrote to Miss Gentle, asking her to bring him to Stamford Hill in Hackney so she could take him to his live with his father in France. Miss Gentle, who had grown very attached to the little boy, packed his carefully-laundered clothes into a parcel in preparation for his journey. She arrived at the rendezvous and, at the appointed time, reluctantly handed him over to his mother.

Over the next couple of hours, several witnesses saw mother and son strolling happily together but, that evening, Louisa took Manfred into the ladies' toilets at Dalston Junction Station and smashed his head and face with a brick that she had brought with her for that purpose.

She then placed a cloth over his mouth to make sure that he was dead; and, to prevent him from being identified, she stripped him naked, wrapped him in a new shawl, and dumped him behind one of the toilets. Her task complete, she cheerfully boarded a train to Brighton for a romantic weekend away with Eudore.

Within half an hour, an unfortunate lady stumbled across the little body, and, by the following morning, the story of her gruesome find appeared in the press. When Miss Gentle read the article, she became very uneasy, and, a few days later, she told the police that she feared the child might be Manfred Masset. She was taken to identify the body and shown a parcel of clothes that had been retrieved from the left luggage office, both of which confirmed her suspicions.

On being arrested, Louisa claimed that she had placed the boy in the care of two sisters, who, for a one-off payment, had agreed to adopt him. She could not, though, produce a receipt for the payment, nor any proof of the sisters' existence; and the jury at her trial took only a few minutes to find her guilty of murder.

Petitions for a reprieve came from both sides of the Channel, and a large group of French governesses wrote directly to Queen Victoria, asking her to intervene. Her barrister also continued to argue that the evidence was circumstantial and, when Louisa complained that the judge's summing up had been biased, the Home Secretary released a statement to the press, assuring the public that he would carefully consider every aspect of the case and verdict. Having done so, he concluded that there were no grounds for a reprieve and Louisa was hanged in Newgate Prison on 9th January 1900.

# Chapter 11 – Wicked Stepmothers

In the early years of the nineteenth century, Jacob and Wilhelm Grimm published a collection of German folktales, which were translated into English and gained a wide readership. Far from being sanitised fairy stories of handsome princes and happy endings, these gory tales of violence, murder and cannibalism were filled with archetypal villains, one of whom was the 'wicked stepmother.'

In an era when death in childbirth was commonplace, widowed fathers were expected to find a new wife to care for their children. Consequently, countless women became stepmothers and, while the majority, of course, bore no resemblance to their fictional counterparts, a few who gained notoriety confirmed the evil image in the public imagination.

Although not officially married, Harriet Parker agreed to care for Robert Blake's children when, in 1846, he left his wife to become her live-in lover. Blake had no intention, though, of remaining faithful to Harriet and, much to her chagrin, he openly visited other women and regularly frequented brothels.

On New Year's Eve 1848, he came home from work and ordered Harriet to bring his supper quickly as he had made plans to go to the theatre with a friend. When she offered to go with them, he replied that she was not welcome, which so annoyed her that she decided to tag along anyway. She trailed him through several pubs until he told her to go home as he was on his way to meet a prostitute. Incensed, she ranted at him so wildly that he silenced her with a punch in the face. Seething with rage, she swore that she would have her revenge and, hurrying home, she smothered his two young children while they slept.

Without the slightest trace of remorse, she woke her neighbours to tell them what she had done, adding that she had been planning to kill the children for several months and was now ready to hand herself in to the police. When a policeman arrived, she repeated her confession, telling him that she was so angry with Robert Blake that she could have killed a thousand children and that she hoped that she would be hanged rather than transported.

At her trial, Blake made a very poor impression on the jury when he admitted that he had often been unfaithful. Although he denied that he had taunted Harriet about his infidelities, the jury, in returning a guilty verdict, recommended mercy in view of his excessive provocation. The judge was far less sympathetic, stating that there was no excuse for killing innocent children to gain revenge on their father, and, as he donned the black cap and pronounced the death sentence, he remarked that he hoped that justice would be served.

Harriet accepted the sentence with resignation, and, expressing deep remorse, she told the prison chaplain, Reverend Davies, that hanging was a just and deserved punishment. On the 25th February, she stayed awake praying and reading the Bible until six o'clock in the morning when Davies arrived with the warders to lead her to the gallows. She thanked the prison staff for their kindness and, stepping towards the noose, said firmly, 'May the Lord have mercy on my soul!'

Harriet's monstrous crime undoubtedly merited a severe sentence but, once again, the randomness of justice is apparent when her case is compared to that of another 'wicked stepmother', Mary Seago.

The daughter of a workhouse master, Mary was a widow with one young son, Tommy, when she married a widower, Seago, the father of two children, Ann and Billy. From the start, the marriage was characterised by alcohol-fuelled violence, and, while their parents fought and drank, the children were so neglected and undernourished that they occasionally spent time in the workhouse. None of them enjoyed a happy childhood but Tommy fared better than Ann and Billy as he was spared the severe corporal punishment that Mary regularly inflicted on her stepchildren.

One afternoon in May 1854, Tommy told his mother that his stepfather had hit him because six-year-old Billy had got him into trouble. Without bothering to find out what had happened, Mary angrily pushed Billy off the box on which he was sitting and sent him straight to bed. He did as he was told but, as it was the middle of the day, he soon got up again without asking Mary's permission. As a punishment for his disobedience, she thrashed him with a strap before plunging him fully clothed into a wooden tub of water. She scrubbed and hit him so ferociously that Tommy was horrified and, at the first opportunity, he gently helped his little stepbrother out of the tub, took off his wet clothes and gently tucked him back into bed.

Minutes later, Mary ordered him to get up again to clean a tray but he was so weak from the beating that it was difficult for him to obey her. Happily, at that moment, he heard his father knock on the door and, as Ann ran down to let him in, Mary ordered Billy to get back into bed.

When Ann told him what had happened, Seago angrily yelled at Mary and said that he was leaving.

'Go,' she cried, 'and take your bloody children with you,' but, rather than protecting Ann and Billy, he walked out again, leaving them behind.

Billy sat up in bed, which so ignited Mary's temper that she seized him and hurled him across the room, where he hit his head on the corner of a tin box. Still not satisfied, she kicked him viciously, ignoring Tommy's desperate warnings that, if she did not stop, she would kill him.

At length, her rage subsided, and the other children hurried to Billy's aid but he lay lifeless on the floor – a mass of blood and bruises. Suddenly realising that he was not moving, Mary desperately tried to pour brandy down his throat while telling him that she loved him! It was all to no avail. The little boy was dead.

Rather than showing any remorse, Mary ordered the other children to tell no one what had happened, and, wrapping Billy in a blanket, she carried him the hospital where she left him. It was obvious to the doctors that the child had died as the result of a vicious attack, and a policeman was sent to Mary's home to question her.

She said that Billy was a weak, consumptive child, who suffered from a heart complaint, and, calmly showing him the wooden tub, explained to the policeman that she had been washing the 'beloved boy' when he slipped and fell out, cracking his head on the corner of the tin box. Unconvinced, the policeman took her to the station and returned to the house to examine the scene more closely and to question the other children. Observing the extent of the blood spatter and hearing Ann's account of what had happened, he was left in no doubt that Mary was guilty of murder.

Her trial took place in July 1854 in the Old Bailey, where she was ably represented by the barrister, Mr Parry. Dismissing Ann's evidence on the grounds that she was a child and so could not be trusted, Parry said that Mary had bought Billy a penny pie earlier that day, which was proof that she loved him. Unable to deny that she had caused the boy's death, he suggested that her violent outburst was an aberration, and, as murder had never been her intention, he succeeded in reducing the charge to manslaughter.

Her initial sentence was transportation to the colonies but this was almost immediately reduced to imprisonment. Soon after her arrival in Brixton Prison, she was diagnosed with a heart condition which necessitated her permanent removal to the infirmary wing, where her behaviour showed that, contrary to Parry's claim, her violent rage against Billy was anything but a one-off aberration. For the slightest perceived offence, she fell into paroxysms of fury, putting others' lives in danger. One day, for example, when a prison nurse annoyed her, she:

> "...suddenly turned out of bed, wherein she had lain for many weeks, and walked very coolly and stealthily from her own room to the apartment of the nurse, a little way distant. That officer was considerably amazed by Seago's appearance, a la Lady Macbeth, and no less alarmed when she saw her snatch up a knife that lay handy, and brandish it above her head. Fortunately, help was at hand, and Seago was removed to her old quarters, it being impossible to punish one in so delicate a state of health ."[60]

Eventually, as her health was failing, she was released from prison on compassionate grounds. She returned home, took to her bed and died a few days later, leaving few to mourn her passing.

Mary Seago was fortunate to avoid a capital sentence, but, fourteen years later, another wicked stepmother became the last woman to be hanged in public in England.

William Kidder, a greengrocer from Kent, was an honourable and well-meaning man and so, when an illiterate eighteen-year-old servant, Frances, gave birth to his child, he 'did the right thing' and married her. The couple lived happily together, raising their baby, Emma, until news arrived that one of William's former lovers and the mother of his illegitimate child, had died and there was no one to care for his eight-year-old daughter, Louisa.

Again, William did his duty and brought the little girl into his home, much to the annoyance of Frances who bitterly resented the intrusion. Regularly beating Louisa and referring to her as 'Kidder's bastard', she deprived her of food and warm clothing until the neighbours were so alarmed that they reported her to the authorities. The unrepentant Frances was fined for neglect, and, in an effort to improve the situation, William arranged to pay for Louisa to be cared for by a childminder. For a little while, peace was restored until William failed to meet the minder's fee, and poor Louisa was returned to her father.

Some months later, Frances fell from a cart and was left concussed for several hours, after which her hatred of her stepdaughter increased. Neighbours were shocked by the bitterness with which she spoke about the child, and they were even more disconcerted when she said that she would soon be rid of Kidder's bastard.

In August 1867, Frances took Emma and Louisa to visit her parents; and, while there, with an uncharacteristic show of kindness, she offered to take Louisa to the fair. They set off happily together but, as they crossed a bridge over a shallow stream, Frances seized her chance to be rid of the child by grabbing her and forcing her face-down into the water.

Hours passed and Frances' parents wondered why they hadn't returned from fair; and, when William arrived in the evening, he and Frances' father went out to look for them. After a fruitless search, they returned home and, a few minutes later, Frances, drenched and muddy, appeared on the doorstep. In spite of her parents' urgent pleas, she refused to say what had happened to Louisa, which so alarmed William that he sent for a constable.

As Frances still refused to offer an explanation for Louisa's absence, the constable arrested her on suspicion of murder, and, after several hours in custody, she finally came up with a story. Louisa, she said, had taken fright at some horses and had stumbled into the stream and drowned. When asked why her own clothes were wet and muddy, she replied that she had tried to save the child but had been unable to do so. The shallowness of the slow-flowing stream gave lie to her explanation, and, when Louisa's body was found, Frances was charged with her murder.

While in custody, she suffered a series of fits which might have been used to suggest that she was not of sound mind at the time of the killing, but, during her trial at the Maidstone Assizes, her mental state was never mentioned, and she was sentenced to hang.

In the immediate aftermath of the murder, there had been great public antipathy towards her but, once she had been sentenced, she was portrayed as a victim of an unfaithful husband. William's refusal to visit her in prison further damaged his reputation, and, when she was finally hanged, the press condemned the system which had failed her. She was, noted several newspapers, a 'woman of the very lowest order of rational creatures, ignorant, brutal, and debased from her birth'; and, consequently, 'her death may have avenged the law, but it has also shocked and disgusted many more than it will terrify, or deter from the like indulgence of savage instincts.'

Six weeks later, the Capital Punishment Within Prisons Act became law, ending the unseemly spectacle of public hangings.

# Chapter 12 – The Baby Farmers

During the sixty-three years of Queen Victoria's reign, the population of Great Britain increased from twenty-five million in 1837 to forty-one million by 1901, and the number of unmarried mothers rose in proportion to the general rise in the population. Although this led to an increase in the instances of infanticide, the majority of mothers could not contemplate such drastic action and so they were left with the problem of how to care for their illegitimate children while earning a living.

Their difficulties gave rise to an entirely new and lucrative industry of child minders, who placed advertisements in newspapers, offering to care for children for a weekly or monthly fee; or to provide permanent adoption for a one-off payment. The adoption fees ranged from five pounds for a servant to up to two-hundred pounds for a genteel person, with the guarantee of discretion and the promise that the child would be raised in a loving home.

Undoubtedly, many of these minders took their duties seriously and, like Miss Gentle[s], became genuinely fond of the children in their care. Others, though, were solely interested in making a profit as quickly as possible, and went to unconscionable lengths to achieve that end. Some – the 'baby famers' – took in far more children than they could reasonably house, and, once the fees had been collected, they neglected them to the point of letting them starve. Some were astonishingly explicit, implying that, for an extra fee, they could guarantee that babies would not survive for long in their care; others used coded language or claimed to be respectable married ladies who, not having been blessed with children of their own, were eager to provide a home to an unwanted infant.

---

[s] Manfred Massett's minder - See Chapter 10

For years, the sordid practice had attracted little criticism until, in 1865, the body of a four-month-old boy was found wrapped in old newspapers on a roadside near Torre Station in Devon. A post-mortem showed that he had been suffocated four or five days earlier, and investigations soon led the police to an unmarried servant, Mary Harris.

Mary not only admitted that she was the little boy's mother but also gave the police an horrific account of what had happened. Her forty-five-year-old friend, Charlotte Winsor, had offered to help her dispose of the baby, assuring her that it was easily done as she had already dispatched several others by strangulation or suffocation. There was no problem, she added, in disposing of the bodies, as they could be left by the roadside or tossed into the sea.

In effort to save her own skin, Mary Harris altered her story to suggest that she had played no part in the murder; and she agreed to testify against her former friend in return for immunity from prosecution. During Charlotte Winsor's trial, however, Mary's mask of innocence soon began to slip when it was shown that she had tried to kill the boy on three separate occasions, and only Mrs Winsor's intervention had prevented her from succeeding. She had first tried to poison him with ratsbane[t] coated in sugar; she had started to drown him; and had attempted to smother him, but, each time, Mrs Winsor came to his rescue.

Nonetheless, the jury took little more than an hour to find Mrs Winsor guilty and, as the judge pronounced the death sentence, she became so hysterical that it took her several hours to recover. Over the next few weeks, her execution was repeatedly postponed until, much to the annoyance of several judges, the sentence was commuted to life imprisonment.

"What a pedant that doubting lawyer must be who at

---

[t] An arsenical compound used for killing rats.

once caused Charlotte Winsor to be respited," complained Baron Bramwell. "Was it Parke, or Rolfe, and why did not the Chancellor (feeble man!) ask at once the personal opinion of the Judges, and act upon the result?"[61]

Life, however, did indeed mean life for the baby-killer, as she died in prison almost thirty years later. Mary Harris, having turned Queen's Evidence, walked from the court a free woman.

Campaigners hoped that the outrage provoked by the Winsor case would put an end to the baby-famers' practices but, once the trial was over, public interest waned and the whole sorry episode was forgotten.

"It was only," wrote one angry reformer, "while we, following the revolting revelations, were subject to a succession of shocks and kept in pain, that we were thus virtuous. It, was only while our tender feelings were suffering excruciation from the harrowing story of baby torture that we shook in wrath against the torturer...Barely was the trial of the murderess concluded and the court cleared than our fierce indignation subsided from its bubbling and boiling, and quickly settled down to calm and ordinary temperature."[62]

Such was the public's apathy that there was no outcry whatsoever when, a few years later, a child was found dead in a small egg crate in the home Caroline Savill. Even when it was reported that eleven other children were crammed into the same small establishment, the story was given only a few short paragraphs in the papers.

At the child's inquest, it was revealed that some months earlier Mrs Savill, while carrying him upstairs, slipped and fell on top of him, breaking his leg. Whether the accident was due to her being drunk or, as she claimed, a pair of ill-fitting boots, the injury was left untreated until the following morning when Mrs Savill finally called a doctor.

Bizarrely, the lackadaisical doctor said there was nothing to worry about, and he saw no need to stabilise the fracture or to provide analgesia. When the child was found dead in his egg box bed, the same doctor confirmed that his leg was still broken, but stated that death was due to natural causes. Although the inquest jury accepted the doctor's assessment, they asked the coroner to issue some form of censure to prevent Mrs Savill from continuing her trade. The coroner replied that it was not within his power to do so, and, consequently, Mrs Savill carried on taking in children, unhindered by any regulations or inspections. Not until 1870, when the sensational case of the Brixton Baby Farmer hit the headlines, were any serious attempts made to combat the horrors of the trade.

Widowed at the age of twenty-nine in 1864, Margaret Waters took up child-minding as a means of earning a living. Having placed advertisements in the papers, she soon found she had more charges than she could feed, and so, through ignorance rather than malevolence, she slowly let them starve. To silence their hungry cries, she drugged them with opiates and, when they died, she found various means of disposing of the bodies. Sometimes she left them under railway arches or on street corners; and, on more than one occasion, she wrapped them in shawls as though they were still alive, and carried them into the street where she waited for an unsuspecting child to walk by. She then offered the child a penny to hold the baby while she went into a shop, and, once the child had taken the bundle, she disappeared into the crowds. Over six years, she is believed to have killed at least nineteen babies, and that number would surely have been higher were it not for the diligence of one observant Metropolitan policeman.

Sergeant Richard Relf was so concerned about the baby-farmers' activities that he ploughed through their advertisements until he managed to locate one of their correspondents – a musician named Robert Cowen. Cowen told him that his seventeen-year-old daughter, Jeanette, had given birth to a little boy after being raped by a family friend. Apparently more concerned with avoiding a further scandal than with prosecuting the rapist, Cowen decided to have the baby adopted. He answered a newspaper advert and arranged a meeting with a 'Mrs Oliver', who, for a fee, took the baby, John, promising that he would be raised in a loving home.

Relf, determined to locate Mrs Oliver, asked Cowen to write to her again, requesting a further meeting, but the letter was returned to him unopened. Refusing to give up, Relf himself replied to the advert, claiming he had a child whom he wished to put up for adoption; and, within a few days, Mrs Oliver replied and arranged to meet him.

On the day of the meeting, Relf asked Cowen to watch from a distance and to signal to him if Mrs Oliver was the same woman who had taken Jeannette's baby. When Cowen confirmed that this was the case, Relf asked for her address and, as she refused to answer, he secretly followed her to a house on Frederick Place in Brixton.

The next day, he returned to Frederick Place with his landlady, Mrs Guerra, and, entering the house, he demanded to see Jeanette Cowen's baby. When the child was brought in, Mrs Guerra was so aghast at his emaciated state that she accused Mrs Oliver of starving him.

Relf searched the house and found nine equally malnourished and filthy children, some of whom, like little John Cowen, had diarrhoea and appeared so vacant that he was convinced that they had been drugged. The discovery of an open bottle of laudanum confirmed his suspicions; and a large quantity of children's clothing suggested that many more children had passed through the establishment.

Relf sent for the District Medical Officer, Doctor Puckle, who took one look at the children and ordered that they should all be taken to the infirmary of the Lambeth Workhouse.

In the midst of the kerfuffle, 'Mrs Oliver' confessed that her real name was Sarah Ellis, and that she worked for her sister, Margaret Waters, who ran the operation. Margaret Waters was equally co-operative, admitting that she had taken in over forty children but she insisted that John Cowen's emaciation was due to diarrhoea rather than neglect. Neither she nor Sarah Ellis appeared concerned when they were taken into custody, but, a few days later when John Cowen and four other children died in the Lambeth Workhouse, Margaret Waters was horrified to be charged with the little boy's murder.

At her trial, the Brixton surgeon, Edmund Pope, gave evidence that John had died of an effusion of the brain due to repeated overdoses of narcotics. This and the details of the squalor in which the children had been living was sufficient to convince the jury that Margaret Waters was guilty of murder. Her sister, who had not been involved in drugging the children, was convicted on a lesser charge.

Petitioners argued that Margaret had not set out to kill the children, but, in view of the public outrage, the Home Secretary saw no reason to overturn the death sentence. On 11th October 1870 in Horsemonger Lane Prison, Margaret Waters became the first baby-farmer to hang.

The revelations and the public response to the case, prompted politicians to regulate the practice of baby-farming but the subsequent legislation served only to exacerbate the problem. The Infant Life Protection Act of 1872 made it illegal for anyone to accept payment for the care of more than one child under twelve months old, unless they were registered as a foster carer with the local authority. Instead of protecting children, this led unscrupulous baby-farmers to dispose of one child as quickly as possible, so that they could obtain the fee for another.

"If a man who ruins a girl pays down a sum of £20, the boarding home is immune from inspection," wrote Emmeline Pankhurst. "As long as the baby farmer takes only one child at a time, the house cannot be inspected. Of course, the babies die with hideous promptness, often long before the twenty pounds has been spent, and then baby farmers are free to solicit another victim."[63]

The Act failed to save the life of little Reginald Hyde, whose unmarried mother, Mary Hoskins, had placed him the care of a middle-aged widow named Annie Tooke. For a down-payment of twelve pounds and a maintainer of five shillings a week, Mrs Tooke assured the mother that he would be well cared for. It is possible that she initially intended to honour her promise but, within a few months, the baby had become such a burden to her that she smothered him with a pillow and chopped his body into pieces, which she tossed into a millstream.

The unfortunate miller soon stumbled upon the little boy's torso, and a brief search led to the discovery of the rest of the remains. Local people, who had seen Mrs Tooke with the baby, reported that he had gone missing and, within a few days, she was arrested. She immediately made a full confession, which she later retracted in the hope of laying the blame on Reginald's mother. She was found guilty of murder in August 1879, and hanged in a makeshift execution yard in the former hospital in Exeter Gaol.


In spite of the publicity given to the cases of Margaret Water and Annie Tooke, the baby-farming industry continued to flourish across the whole of the United Kingdom and, indeed, across the whole of Europe. One of the most infamous cases occurred in Edinburgh in the autumn of 1888, when little two boys, kicking around a package that they found on wasteland, discovered that it contained the decaying corpse of a baby. In a fright, they ran to find a policeman, who took the bundle to the mortuary for a post-mortem, which revealed that the otherwise healthy boy had been strangled.

As news of the discovery spread through the vicinity, a landlord, James Banks, told the police that several months earlier he had let a room to a 'Mr and Mrs Macpherson', who were caring for a baby girl named Violet. When the baby vanished, Mr Banks had asked what had become of her, to which Mrs Macpherson replied that she had been adopted and they had made some money from the transaction.

Banks' story caught the police's attention as they were already investigating a missing child named Violet Tomlinson. Her grandmother, who reported her disappearance, explained that her daughter had advertised for someone to care for her illegitimate child until she was able to arrange a full adoption. 'Mrs Burns' answered the advertisement, offering to take care of the child for a fee of two pounds until her sister, Mrs McPherson, could arrange to adopt her. Miss Tomlinson handed Violet over to Mrs Burns and, in the days that followed, her mother went several times to Mrs Burns' home in the hope of seeing her but, on each occasion, she was met with excuses and refused admission.

When the police located Mrs Burns, they were struck by her awkward behaviour. On being asked to open a cupboard, she claimed the key was missing, but when policeman found it, she panicked and cried out, "I did it!" The policeman opened the cupboard and found Violet's body and indications that another baby had also been stored there.

The ensuing inquiry revealed that 'Mrs Burns' was an alias of twenty-nine-year-old Jessie King, an illiterate woman of low intelligence, who lived with a married man, Thomas Pearson, thirty years her senior. Pearson, a drunk and a bully, had left his wife and family to move in with Jessie when she was pregnant with another man's child, and, from the start, he exerted a powerful influence over her.

They began taking in babies as a means of making money and, when the babies cried, they gave them whisky, which, according to Jessie, was what killed Violet Tomlinson. The baby found on the wasteland was another of their charges – Alexander Gunn; and Jesse confessed that another child, Walter Campbell, had also died while in their care but his body was never found.

When the couple was arrested, Jessie asserted that she had acted alone and Pearson was unaware of what she had done. Her lover failed to repay her loyalty and instead agreed to give evidence against her in return for immunity from prosecution. Found guilty of murder, she was sentenced to death and, after a failed attempt to strangle herself, she was executed in Edinburgh on 11th March 1889 – the last woman to be hanged in the city.

Of all the baby-farmers none was more prolific or more despised than Amelia Dyer, who is believed to have killed up to four hundred babies. In truth, at the time of her trial in 1896, there was little about her to win public sympathy, as her fearsome features reflected the horrific crime with which she was charged, and she could use neither poverty nor ignorance as an excuse for her malevolence.

After a comfortable childhood and a good education as the daughter of a master shoemaker, she served an apprenticeship as a corset-maker before marrying George Thomas at the age of twenty-five. She would later allege that her husband, who was several decades her senior, treated her cruelly and squandered the money that she had inherited from her father.

In the late 1850s, she trained as a nurse and, while working in a hospital, made the acquaintance of a midwife, Ellen Dane, who told her that many unmarried mothers paid strangers to care for their children. It occurred to Amelia that baby-farming would be far more profitable than nursing, and, when her husband died, she decided to go into the business. Thanks to her nursing experience, she had no problem attracting clients as she arranged to care for pregnant girls during their confinement and, afterwards, for an extra free, she would take care of their babies.

The babies were neglected, starved and plied with opiates to keep them quiet. If they took too long to die, she happily helped them on their way, until a local doctor, alarmed by the number of death certificates that she asked him to sign, reported his concerns to the police. Amelia was arrested but, charged with neglect rather than murder, she was imprisoned for only six months before being released to resume her macabre trade.

Determined not to make the same mistake again, she dispensed with the need for death certificates by disposing of the bodies herself; and, for extra security against detection, she adopted a series of aliases and regularly moved house. Whenever it seemed that her crimes were about to be discovered, she attempted suicide and committed herself to a lunatic asylum. Whether or not the suicide attempts were genuine is open to question, as a woman who could kill so many infants would surely have been capable of arranging her own demise if that were her true intention.

As is so often the case with serial killers, murder became so easy for her that she grew increasingly careless. No longer taking the trouble to dispose of the corpses quickly, she left them lying around her house, filling the place with the stench of decay, until she found the time to toss them into the river.

On March 31$^{st}$ 1896, a waterman opened a package that he had found floating in the Thames, and discovered that it contained the rotting corpse of a strangled baby girl. The remains were wrapped in brown paper, addressed to 'Mrs Thomas, Piggott's Road Lower Caversham'.

By then, Amelia, alias Mrs Thomas, had taken in two more babies – Doris Marmon and Harry Simmons – unaware that the net was closing in around her. In order to ensure they had the right address, the police asked two women to pose as potential customers and, when Amelia answered the door, they burst in to arrest her. Although no babies were found in the house, the stench was overwhelming; and, when the bodies of Doris and Harry were fished from the river, Amelia Dyer was charged with murder. She not only confessed to Doris' murder but also told the police that they would recognise her handy-work by the white tape that she always wrapped around the necks of her victims. Over the next few weeks, several more dead babies, bound with white tape, were found in the river.

While awaiting trial, Amelia tried to strangle herself before pleading not guilty by reason of insanity. Dr Forbes Winslow examined her and concluded that she had inherited madness from her mother, who was prone to violent outbursts and had been certified insane. In response to his questions, Amelia claimed to have no recollection of the dead children although she often heard voices and saw the spirits of her dead son and mother.

"I considered," Forbes Winslow said at her trial, "that she was a person of unsound mind, suffering from delusions and hallucinations. She was suffering from melancholia and delusional insanity. There was no excitement, but there was depression and there were delusions. The prisoner made no attempt to feign insanity. I examined her to see whether she was shamming insanity. I came to the conclusion that she was not. She said that very often she got into a depressed condition, and that voices spoke to her and told her to take her own life, and that she had made several attempts to do that, but had been prevented."[64]

Oddly, though, while claiming to have no recollection of murdering the babies, she could recall in detail her suicide attempts and periods of incarceration in various asylums.

Other doctors concurred with Forbes Winslow, one stating that, while in the Bristol Asylum, she had rushed at him with a poker and threatened to smash his skull. Another, who had treated her following a suicide attempt, also attested that she was insane. She had told him that she had no control over her violent outbursts, remarking, "My only wonder is, I did not murder all in the house when I have had all these awful temptations on me."[65]

Neither the judge, Mr Justice Hawkins, nor the jury believed the doctors' assessments, and, when a guilty verdict was returned, there was no recommendation for mercy.

"Not a voice was raised for her," the press reported. "The utterly despicable character of Mrs Dyer's crime may be judged from the fact that not a single word has been raised by the public or the press on behalf of a commutation of her sentence to penal servitude on the ground that she is a woman. She has gone to the gallows unpitied and hated. For Mrs Dyer no one ever asked for mercy, and no hope has been held out since her plea of insanity failed."[66]

Showing neither remorse nor the least concern for her victims' families, Amelia Dyer was hanged on 10th June 1896, and buried in an unmarked grave within the confines of Newgate Prison.

The Dyer case had created such outrage that the Attorney General was put under pressure to introduce a new Infant Life Protection Act to regulate the baby-farmers; but it also led to widespread condemnation of mothers who placed their babies in the care of strangers. Failing to comprehend the desperate circumstances in which many young women found themselves, a censorious public denounced those whom they deemed responsible for enabling the baby-farmers to continue to trade.

"Far is it, alas from being always necessary to deceive mothers in order to secure their children's charge," wrote Benjamin Waugh indignantly. "There are infamous creatures, mere she-things, who look out for foul and dishonourable people to consign their children to...While cannibal mothers, when an unwanted child is born, are said 'to put it back again' in a meal, English mothers put their unwanted children back by a process of which the cannibal would be ashamed, but which, happily for the comparison, her eye does not actually see."[67]

Waugh was clearly unaware that hundreds of women, like Violet Tomlinson's grandmother, were desperate to maintain contact with the children, and it was thanks to them that some of the baby-farmers' crimes came to light. One tragic case was that of a caring mother, Florence Jones, who had done everything in her power to find a good home for her illegitimate daughter, twenty-one-month-old, Selina Ellen. She had carefully chosen a number of child-minders, who had treated the little girl well, but when she could no longer afford to keep up the payments, she realised that Selina would have a better life if she were permanently adopted.

In the summer of 1899, Florence saw an advertisement in the paper from a Mr and Mrs Hewetson, promising a permanent home for a child for a one-off payment of five pounds. Reluctant as she was to part with the child, she arranged to meet Mrs Hewetson at Woolwich Station.

Although the meeting went well and Mrs Hewetson made a favourable impression, Florence became so distressed at the thought of leaving her baby that Mrs Hewetson assured her that she and her mother could visit Selina whenever they wished, and, if Florence's circumstances improved, she could take her back home. Greatly relieved, Florence agreed to bring the baby the following week, and, in return, Mrs Hewetson promised to show her the Hammersmith home where her child would live.

As agreed, the next week, they met at Charing Cross Station and travelled together to Hammersmith but, when they arrived at the house, Mrs Hewetson said they could not go inside, as workmen were busy renovating the property. Having only three pounds to her name, Florence handed over the baby and the money, promising to pay the outstanding two pounds when she visited Selina a few days later. Mrs Hewetson seemed happy with the arrangement and agreed that she would soon be in touch to arrange the visit. Florence, feeling reassured, left Selina in her care, and returned to her parents' home in Croydon.

Days passed but when Florence heard nothing from Mrs Hewetson, she decided to go to Hammersmith to find out why she had not been in contact. To her astonishment, the occupants of the house had never heard of anyone called Hewetson, neither had the local shopkeepers nor any of the neighbours. In desperation, Florence reported her troubles to the police, who discovered that Hewetson was an alias for Ada Chard Williams, who, with her husband, William, had vanished without trace.

With no leads to follow, the police could only remain vigilant in the hope that the child was still alive, but, a few weeks later, a boatman found her little body tightly wrapped in a parcel near Battersea Bridge. An investigation revealed that the parcel was tied with a number of unusual knots, including the 'fisherman's bend', which had been used to bind the bodies of two other children, who had been found strangled and thrown into the Thames some months earlier. Florence faced the heart-breaking task of identifying her dead daughter, while the police stepped up their search for Ada and William Chard Williams, who now faced a charge of murder.

When the murderess read in the press that she was wanted by the police, she was so terrified that she immediately invented a story. She admitted taking Selina but averred that she had then passed her on to another woman and did not know what had become of her. The police raided her Hackney home and arrested her and her husband before carrying out a thorough search of the house and another property in Barnes where the couple had previously resided.

A quantity of children's clothing was found, as well as wrappings and cord, like that which had been used to bind Selina's body; and, from inquiries in the neighbourhood, the police learned that other children, who had been in the Chard Williams' care, had vanished suddenly. Neighbours attested that Ada had frequently beaten the children, and prevented her husband from showing them any kindness.

At their trial in the Old Bailey in December 1899, their defence presented neither witnesses nor evidence; but the judge, Sir Edward Ridley, was particularly keen to discuss the 'fisherman's bend', with which, he assured the court, he was very familiar. The jury retired for only half an hour before finding Ada guilty and, when Ridley passed the death sentence, she calmly replied, 'Thank you, my Lord,' before being led away to Newgate.

William was found not guilty of murder but guilty of being an accessory after the fact, and, after some discussion with the barristers, the judge ordered the jury to acquit him. No sooner had he been released, however, than he was rearrested for fraud.

Ada was hanged on 8th March 1900, gaining the dubious honour of not only being the last woman to be hanged in Newgate Prison[u], but also the last to be hanged during the reign of Queen Victoria.

---

[u] Newgate closed two years later.

# Chapter 13 – The Root of Evil

One of the more macabre side-effects of the increasing population and the migration from the countryside to the towns was that burial sites were so overcrowded that they posed a serious threat to public health. Gravediggers in Leeds Parish Churchyard were forced to smash buried coffins and trample them into the earth to make room for the new additions; and, in London, undertakers were paid to tap into the coffins crammed tightly into church vaults, to release the gasses to prevent them from exploding.

The most grotesque events occurred in London's Enon Chapel, beneath which over twelve hundred bodies were buried between 1822 and 1839, in a space that measured only twelve feet wide by fifty-nine feet in length. The avaricious Baptist minister, W. Howse, was so keen to make money from interments that he took the bodies out of their coffins to pack them in more tightly. His unsuspecting congregation assumed that the proliferation of flies and the overwhelming stench of decay were the result of the chapel being built over a sewer, but, in 1839, when council officers came to replace the sewage system, they discovered, immediately below the floorboards, hundreds of corpses in various states of putrefaction.

The scandal highlighted the problem of a lack of suitable burial sites, and prompted a greater number of private companies to purchase land for cemeteries, wherein the bereaved could lay their loved ones to rest in carefully-tended plots in leafy surroundings. In 1845, the first municipal cemetery opened in Beckett Street in Leeds; and throughout the 1850s and 1860s, legislation led to the creation of other huge municipal cemeteries, in which the dead were honoured with increasingly ornate monuments, the costs of which could be covered by life insurance companies.

Life insurance was not a Victorian innovation but dated back to Roman times when, for a few denarii each month, the insurer would receive sufficient funds to pay for a funeral and grave. With the Romans' departure, the practice went into decline until the end of the seventeenth century when the first Annuity Association was established in Britain. This gave rise to a chilling form of gambling, as anyone could take out a policy on anyone whom they chose. Gamblers placed substantial sums on the lives of sickly-looking strangers or frail and elderly neighbours and, if they died before a certain date, the policy holder could rejoice in his winnings. This distasteful practice continued until 1774, when the Life Assurance Act stipulated that an insurer must have a legitimate interest in the life of the person named on the policy.

For the most part, the policies served only the middle class until the opening of the municipal cemeteries led to a fashion for elaborate funerals among all strata of society. The humiliation of being unable to provide 'a good send-off' for a loved one was made all the more painful by the knowledge that the alternative was an unmarked pauper's grave shared with seven or eight strangers. Consequently, churches, co-operatives and trade unions established burial clubs and life assurance associations, which, for a few pennies a week, ensured a grave and a fitting funeral for the person named on the policy.

In spite of stringent regulations, the schemes were open to abuse by those who saw them as a means of profiting from the death of a relation. Parents of sickly children, for example, could enrol in several burial clubs so that when the child died, they would receive payments from multiple sources. More sinisterly, the schemes gave the unscrupulous a motive for murder when their desire to obtain a pay-out exceeded their concern for their families.

In 1847, Mary Anne Milner poisoned her aged mother-in-law to collect a burial club payment, and her crime would have gone undetected had she not decided to repeat it a short time later. On June 16th, she invited her sister-in-law, Hannah Jickels, and her daughter, Ellen, to breakfast at her cottage in the Lincolnshire village of Barnetby Le Wold. She served them pancakes laced with arsenic, which they ate before returning home.

Later that morning, Hannah came back to tell Mary Anne that Ellen was so ill that she believed that the pancakes had been poisoned. Without denying the allegation, Mary Anne silently disposed of the remains of the meal and, two hours later, news reached her that both Hannah and Ellen were dead.

A vigilant doctor observed that their symptoms were identical to those which afflicted Mary Anne's mother-in-law, which was seen as sufficient evidence to warrant her arrest. She stood trial at the Lincoln Assizes and, although there were neither witnesses nor any concrete evidence, the jury was convinced of her guilt and she was sentenced to death.

Much to the embarrassment of the authorities, Mary Anne avoided the gallows by hanging herself in her cell. The prison governor announced that her sentence had been carried out within the confines of the prison, but, when a warder leaked the story to the press, the governor was forced to withdraw his statement and admit the truth.

Less than a year later, a similar case occurred in Essex where Mary May lived in a cramped home with her husband, Robert; two children from a previous marriage; and two lodgers, one of whom was her half-brother, forty-five-year-old 'Spratty' Watts. Unbeknown to Spratty, Mary registered him with a burial club, and, two weeks later, he suffered a severe bout of vomiting and diarrhoea from which he never recovered. With unseemly haste, Mary had him interred in a pauper's grave, then asked a local rector,

Reverend Wilkins, to confirm that he had been healthy up to the time of his death to enable her to claim the burial club money.

The rector was so disturbed by her behaviour that he reported the matter to the police. Spratty's body was exhumed and, when his stomach was found to contain a substantial quantity of arsenic, Mary was arrested and sent for trial at the Essex Assizes. In spite of her protestations of innocence, she was found guilty and sentenced to hang. Shortly before her execution, she made a full confession and added that she had been influenced by the story of Sarah Chesham[v]. After her death on 19th July 1848, the press printed a rumour that she had also murdered her first husband and several of her children, but there is no evidence to substantiate this allegation.

In February 1863, Alice Holt entered the office of the Wesleyan Assurance Society, armed with a doctor's certificate of good health for her mother, Mary Bailey, whose life she wished to insure for twenty-six pounds. The officials agreed to the policy at a premium of six pence a week, unaware that Mary Bailey was ill, and Alice had persuaded a friend to impersonate her for the medical examination.

Alice returned to the home that she shared with her common law husband, George Holt, and her mother, who soon went into a rapid decline. The dutiful daughter sent for a surgeon, who provided her with medication, and, when he had left, she sent for a medical officer from the Stockport Infirmary without telling him that the surgeon had already visited.

Clearly, she hoped to obtain sufficient medicines to overdose her mother but, when that plain failed, she resorted to buying arsenic. Claiming that her mother's room was plagued with vermin, she scattered the powder

---

[v] See Chapter 14

around her bed, and mixed what was left into a glass of warm water and brandy. Mrs Bailey, seeing that the drink looked gritty, initially refused to drink it, but, when Alice assured her that it only contained the medicines left by the doctor, she swallowed it down…and, by the next morning, she was dead.

As no one suspected foul play, Mary Bailey was duly buried and, when three months had passed without further ado, Alice had every reason to believe that the murder would go undiscovered. What she had failed to anticipate was that the Wesleyan Assurance Company had carried out an investigation and discovered that the medical certificate had been obtained under false pretences.

In view of the fraud, Mary Bailey's body was exhumed and, when it was found to be 'saturated' with arsenic, Alice was arrested and sent for trial at the Chester Assizes. A woman who thought nothing of murdering her mother had even fewer qualms about casting the blame onto her common law husband. Holt, she told her barrister, had previously threatened to set fire to her mother's bed and to poison her with strychnine.

No one believed her story, and Alice was sentenced to hang, but, as she revealed that she was pregnant, the execution was delayed for six months until after the baby was born. Eventually, she faced the inept hangman, William Calcraft, who had failed to check that the trap door was in good working order. As he pulled on the lever, it only partially opened, leaving Alice writhing on the rope for several minutes before choking to death.

Elizabeth Pinckard did not need to go to the trouble of taking out a life insurance policy on her husband's stepmother, Bess, as, in the event of her death, her substantial funds would pass to her stepson – Elizabeth's husband, John. Elizabeth's only problem was that it might be some time before John received his inheritance, as fifty-two-year-old Bess was only a year older than Elizabeth herself, and she happened to be in excellent health.

There was only one solution, Elizabeth decided as she carefully plotted to kill her, and it must be done at a time when neither her husband nor her father-in-law were at home. The perfect opportunity presented itself in October 1851, when John and his father set off to sell a horse at the Daventry Michaelmas Fair.

As soon as her husband had left, Elizabeth sent her maid on errand to allow herself time to hurry across the village to her mother-in-law's cottage. There, she struck Bess a fatal blow with a mallet before tying a tape around her neck and hanging her from a hook on the ceiling, to create the impression that she had committed suicide. With consummate coolness, she then raced home and changed her dress before the maid returned and joined her for lunch. As they ate, she chatted about joining her husband in Daventry, until suddenly a labourer burst through the door, announcing that her mother-in-law was dead by her own hand.

Doctor Sharman was summoned to the cottage and instantly realised that this was a case of murder not suicide. The tape around Bess' neck had snapped, so she was lying dead on the floor but neither her neck nor her features showed any signs of strangulation. Moreover, he said ironically, it was highly unlikely that a woman intent on hanging herself would first strike her own face with such force that the wall behind her was spattered with blood.

When a policeman told Elizabeth that Bess had been murdered, she panicked and implicated herself by her overblown protestations of innocence. She had no motive for murder, she declared, as she and her husband had plenty of money.

Witnesses told a different story. One had seen Elizabeth leaving home soon after the maid departed; another had seen her crossing the village; and a third had heard a cry of 'murder' and the sound of something being dragged across floor, just before Elizabeth emerged from her mother-in-law's cottage.

Tried and found guilty at the Moot Hall in Daventry, she made a full confession and became the last woman in to be hanged in public in Northamptonshire. Little could be said in her favour in view of the fact that she not only murdered an innocent woman but also, by portraying her death as suicide, she might have denied her a Christian burial. She did, however, accept her punishment with resignation, and, as the Northampton Mercury reported:

> "On the fatal morning, she attended prayers in the chapel; when the hymn was being sung her voice was heard above the rest. She went with perfect indifference to execution."

Even this created controversy as, four years later, her ignominious end was used by one Member of Parliament as an argument against the death penalty. The fact that she appeared not to suffer but accepted her fate 'with perfect indifference' was, he said, evidence that 'the punishment of death is not an effective punishment.'

One of the most callous murders for money occurred in Scotland in 1849, when twenty-five-year-old Margaret Hamilton poisoned her sister-in-law, Jean Black. The widowed Jean had been working as a maidservant for Reverend Campbell in Edinburgh when she was seduced by her employer and became pregnant. Campbell had the decency to acknowledge his paternity and, although he was dismissed from his parish, he provided Jean with a financial settlement of twenty pounds for the child's upbringing[w].

Jean returned to her mother's home where her sister-in-law nursed her through her confinement. A healthy baby was born, and, while Jean was still recovering,

---

[w] Approximately £2000 in today's values.

Margaret went to the Bank of Scotland and tried to withdraw her twenty pounds. On being told that she could not do so without the account holder's permission, she forged Jean's signature and withdrew the full amount.

No sooner had Margaret left the bank than she realised that, once Jean recovered, she would notice that the money was missing and would guess who had taken it. Her only solution was to ensure that Jean would never recover, and so she began plying her with arsenic in the guise of a calomel purgative prescribed by the doctor. For a fortnight she administered the poison in ever-increasing doses until Jean was so ill that she asked Margaret to fetch a doctor. Margaret promised to do so, but it was too late, as, by the following morning, her sister-in-law was dead.

Margaret was obviously a very inept murderess whose avarice blinded her to the likely consequences of her actions. Other members of the family asked what had happened to Jean's money and, when inquiries were made at the bank, Margaret was identified as the thief and the forger. This led to calls for a post-mortem, and, when arsenic was discovered in Jean's remains, murder was added to the list of charges.

In spite of all the evidence, the jury at Margaret's trial came to a startling conclusion. While it was likely that she was guilty of forgery and murder, they said, theft had not been proved, and, therefore, she should be acquitted of all charges. When the astounded judge, Lord Cockburn, asked them to explain how they came to this bizarre decision, they deliberated again before replying that it was 'in consequence of the first charge of theft not having been proved, which they believe in a great measure led to the commission of the subsequent crime.'[68] In other words, since she was alleged to have committed murder to conceal theft, if theft had not been proved, there was no motive for murder.

Lord Cockburn dismissed their logic as ludicrous and sentenced Margaret to hang. On 31st January 1850, a crowd of twenty-thousand people gathered outside the Glasgow courthouse to witness her execution. When the noose was placed around her neck, she fainted in terror, and had to be supported until the trapdoor opened and she dropped to her death.

Margaret Hamilton could be forgiven for failing to realise that she would not be allowed to withdraw money without the account holder's permission, as the average Victorian worker earned so little that he or she seldom had any contact with a bank. Those who were able to amass some savings might invest in a Post Office savings account, but the majority kept their meagre income in a safe place within their home.

When cash was in short supply, possessions acquired such significant value that wills often comprised detailed lists of pots, pans and other household items that were to be left to specific beneficiaries. Even where no will had been written, family members were told in advance what they were to receive; and, in many cases, items were labelled with the name of the person to whom they would be bequeathed. Lizzie Pearson of Gainford near Durham, for example, had been told that her Aunt Jane, who had always treated her like her own daughter, intended to leave her all her furniture. When Lizzie left home and married a labourer, John Pearson, she and her aunt remained close; and Lizzie was happy for Jane when she, too, found happiness in marrying a groom, John Watson.

In 1874, Aunt Jane died, and her widower took in a lodger, George Smith, to help cover his rent and expenses. A few months later, when seventy-four-year-old Watson contracted pneumonia, Lizzie also moved in to care for him, bringing her husband and child with her. According to his physician, Dr Homfray, it was thanks to Lizzie's tender ministrations that her uncle made a full recovery.

Although he was restored to health, Watson was no longer able to work, and, as money was in short supply, the lodger advised him to sell off some of his late wife's furniture. Alarmed by the thought that her long-awaited inheritance was slipping away, Lizzie asked Dr Homfray to prescribe a powder to relieve her uncle's constipation. The doctor obliged and, just four hours later, Watson's limbs began jerking uncontrollably and, within a few minutes, he was dead.

Before his body was cold, Lizzie stripped the room of furnishings and linen so that, by the time that Dr Homfray arrived, all that was left was the corpse lying on a bare bedframe from which the mattress and sheets had been removed. Homfray was so shocked that he insisted on carrying out a post-mortem, which revealed nothing untoward beyond a reddening of the gut lining and an unidentifiable liquid in the stomach. He diligently preserved the stomach contents and sent them for analysis to the renowned Dr Thomas Scattergood at the Leeds School of Medicine.

On discovering that the specimen contained strychnine and Prussian blue, Scattergood asked the Gainford police to search the village for any poisons to which Lizzie might have had access. It soon transpired that she had bought Battle's Vermin Killer – a rodenticide consisting of Prussian blue and strychnine.

When Lizzie was found guilty of murder at the Durham Assizes, she desperately tried to escape execution by claiming to be pregnant. A medical examination showed that this was not the case and, on 3rd August 1875, she walked calmly to the scaffold where William Marwood was waiting.

# Chapter 14 – Serial Killers

According to *Chambers Dictionary,* a serial killer is 'a person who murders several victims over a period; often killing the victims in the same way.' It is, therefore, a mistake to claim, as has often been said, that Jack the Ripper was the first modern serial killer in Britain, as throughout the 1840s – forty years before Jack's killing spree – a number of murderesses were hanged for having poisoned multiple victims. In each case, as the double jeopardy principle was operant,[x] suspects was tried for only one murder, so that, in the event of their being found innocent, they could be immediately re-arrested and tried for the murder of a different victim.

Ironically, several serial killers would have escaped justice if they had selected only one or two victims. Moreover, most had little to gain from their subsequent murders, which suggests that they were driven to go on killing solely by an addiction to the sense of power that murder gave them.

At the age of thirty-eight, poor Betty Haslam had lived through so many misfortunes, including the deaths of her first husband and three of her children. Fortune seemed to have turned in her favour, though, when she married a widower, Harry Eccles, in 1841. The first year of her marriage passed without incident. Harry earned a reasonable living, working from Monday to Friday in a mill in Manchester, where he lodged on weekdays, returning home to Betty in Bolton at weekends. His two sons, fifteen-year-old William and thirteen-year-old Richard, worked in local factories; while Betty remained at home, caring for her two youngest children: Annie and Mary.

---

[x] Double jeopardy meant that a person could not be tried twice for the same crime. The principle was in use until 2005.

Twenty months after the wedding, the neighbours' hearts went out to poor Betty when ten-year-old Annie suddenly died. In view of the deaths of her other children, they advised her to ask for a post-mortem to find out if the family was blighted by a hereditary illness. The grieving mother replied that she could not bear the thought of having her child cut open, and instead she accepted a payment from her stepsons' factory to cover the cost of the funeral.

A fortnight later, William came home for lunch in perfect health but, on returning to work, he felt so ill that the foreman sent him back home to recover. On the way, he collapsed in the street and had to be helped to his door by a kindly stranger, whom Betty assured that he would be fine once he had eaten. A few hours later he was dead.

Wasting no time, Betty returned to the factory to ask for a further fifty shillings to bury the boy, but his employers were astounded by his sudden death and reported their concerns to the coroner. The coroner ordered a post-mortem and the exhumations of Betty's other children. William's viscera were found to contain a large amount of arsenic and, although the bodies of two of the other children were too decayed to provide any evidence, the third was also found to be riddled with poison.

The police were convinced that Betty had killed several other members of her family but, at the Liverpool Assizes, she stood on trial solely for William's murder. When the jury returned a guilty verdict, the judge told Betty that she had committed one of the greatest atrocities in the annals of crime and he had no hesitation in sentencing her to death. She was hanged on 6th May 1843, outside Kirkdale Prison in Liverpool.

Only three months later, a second serial murderess was led to the gallows in Bedford after carelessly disposing of two unwanted husbands and her child.

Morality was not a strong feature of Sarah Dazley's childhood, for, while her father was locked in a debtors' prison, her mother indulged herself with several other lovers. Sarah followed her example and was anything but a blushing bride when, at the age of nineteen, she married Simeon Mead. Her marriage vows did not prevent her from continuing her amorous endeavours, and it was probably to escape the attentions of a lover that, two years after the wedding, she and Simeon moved a few miles away to Tadlow in south Cambridgeshire.

Soon after their arrival in Tadlow, Sarah gave birth to a little boy, Jonah, whose death a few months later plunged his father into a deep depression. Simeon's mourning continued unabated until his death in October 1840, leaving neighbours to surmise that grief that killed him.

Within weeks of his death, the same neighbours were shocked to see Sarah flirting in public with a young labourer, William Dazley, and they were more astonished when, only four months later, she and Dazley were married. Once again, though, marriage failed to curb Sarah's promiscuity, and, while she toyed with other lovers, the once-cheerful William regularly sat dejectedly drowning his sorrows in a local tavern. Sarah constantly upbraided him for his excessive drinking until his patience was exhausted and he angrily struck her. Shaking with rage, Sarah ran to the home of her most recent lover, William Waldock, to tell him that her husband had hit her and that she would kill anyone who ever dared to strike her again.

Days later, Dazley fell ill with griping pains and vomiting but the doctor, whom Sarah summoned, saw no cause for alarm. Ann Mead, Sarah's sister-in-law by her first marriage, took good care of him, bringing his meals and medication until he began to recover. One day, though, he refused his pills, telling Ann that they tasted different from those that she usually gave him. To reassure him, Ann swallowed one, which persuaded him that he had been over cautious; and, a few hours later, they both vomited.

At around the same time, a neighbour saw Sarah replacing the doctor's pills with what she claimed was a natural remedy; and, soon afterwards, when Ann also noticed her fidgeting with the medication, she explained that the doctor had told her to increase the dosage. Over the next few days, William's agonies intensified and, when he died on 30th October 1843, Sarah refused to allow the doctor to perform a post-mortem.

Barely was her husband's body laid to rest in the churchyard before Sarah was seen gallivanting with William Waldock. When, with indecent haste and much to the horror of his friends, Waldock announced that he and the widow were to be married, neighbours warned him that she had already lost two husbands and it was rumoured that she played a part in their deaths. On hearing the gossip, the County Coroner, Mr Eyre Eagle, ordered the exhumation of the bodies of both of her husbands and her baby. Although Simeon's remains were too decayed to produce any evidence, arsenic was found in those of William Dazley and baby Jonah.

Before the autopsy results were announced, Sarah fled to London but she was soon apprehended and taken back to Bedford Prison. In a desperate effort to extricate herself, she invented the most unlikely story, claiming that she had poisoned Dazley when she discovered that he had murdered her first husband and her baby.

The tale was so preposterous that a jury took less than half an hour to find her guilty of murder. Unrepentant to the end, Sarah Dazley was hanged in front of a crowd of ten-thousand people on 5th August 1843.

Twelve months later, when thirty-one-year-old Eliza Joyce followed her to the gallows, the crowd could only wonder what had compelled this 'mild and not uninteresting looking woman' to murder two children and attempt to murder a third for no apparent reason.

In 1841, Eliza married a recently-widowed market gardener, William Joyce, the father of five children whose ages ranged from one to thirteen years. The arrangement seemed to suit all parties; and there were no pressing financial concerns as William's income enabled him to employ a servant and an apprentice.

Seven months after the wedding, William's youngest child, Emma, died; and, three months later, Eliza gave birth to a daughter, Ann. In spite of her healthy appearance, the baby survived for only three weeks; and, just eight months later, William's eldest son and namesake also fell ill with stomach pains and vomiting.

At first, William had no reason to believe that his wife was involved in the children's deaths but, when a chemist mentioned that Eliza had recently purchased arsenic, he suddenly started to realise what was happening. He raced home and found the sachet, which he returned to the chemist to ask him to weigh it to see if any had been used. Once the chemist had confirmed that a portion was missing, William went back to his son's bedside, where he learned that Eliza had been plying the boy with medicine. Without a word to his wife, he summoned a surgeon and told him that he feared that his son was being poisoned.

An analysis of the vomit confirmed William's fears, and, at his request, Eliza was arrested. During her absence, the boy recovered but, when she appeared in court, the jury could find no motive for murder and accepted her defence counsel's explanation that her stepson must have taken the arsenic by accident.

Convinced of Eliza's guilt, William refused to allow her to return home, and, having nowhere else to go, she was forced to seek shelter in the Boston Workhouse. While there, she became seriously ill and, believing that she was dying, she confessed to having deliberately poisoned her stepson with arsenic and having killed the other two children with laudanum. The only explanation she offered was that it was 'troublesome' to bring children into a 'troublesome world.'

Having unburdened herself, Eliza made a remarkable recover, only to find herself arrested for murder. Her confession was read out at the Lincoln Summer Assizes and she was hanged on 2nd August 1844.

Throughout her adolescence, Sarah Dimond had gained a fearful reputation for her violent temper and blatant promiscuity. By the age of eighteen, she had given birth to two illegitimate children and was earning her living as a prostitute when she became pregnant again. The clergyman, whom she claimed had fathered her child, paid a seventeen-year-old youth, Henry Freeman, to marry her. For the next seven years, Henry treated the child – James – as his own son, until the little boy suddenly fell ill and died.

A surgeon, who examined the body, was unable to say what had killed him but, when he recommended a post-mortem, the coroner replied that it would be an unnecessary expense and told him to record that death was due to natural causes. The following month, December 1843, twenty-four-year-old Henry also died, and, in spite of his youth and previous good health, the same coroner saw no need for an investigation.

Sarah obtained twenty pounds from the burial club and spent it all in London before returning to her family home in Bridgewater in Somerset. Her brother, Charles, was most put out by her reappearance but, as their mother insisted on welcoming her back, there was nothing he could do to prevent her from staying. A few months later, when Mrs Dimond died, Charles ordered his sister to leave, but instead she bought threepence worth of arsenic and sprinkled it onto his meals.

As soon as he fell ill, Charles sent for Dr Edward England Philips, who recognised the similarity between his symptoms and those of his late mother. When, therefore, Charles died on New Year's Eve 1844, he removed the viscera and sent them to Mr Herepath in Bristol for analysis. As England Philips had expected, the stomach contained so much arsenic that the coroner ordered the exhumation of Charles' body and that of his mother. The two coffins were carried into the church, where they were opened in the presence of the coroner and an inquest jury, after which the organs were removed for further examination.

The entire village packed into the schoolroom for the subsequent inquest, during which the medical evidence was sufficient to persuade the jury that Sarah Freeman was guilty of murder. While she was awaiting trial, the coroner ordered the exhumations of the bodies of Henry and James Freeman, and, as these also contained arsenic, rumours ran rife that Sarah had poisoned many other people, including five children from one family, all of whom died soon after she had visited.

Throughout her trial for the murder of Charles Dimond, Sarah insisted she was innocent and attempted to cast the blame onto another brother. The jury saw through her lies and, when a guilty verdict was returned, she was sentence to hang. In the days prior to her execution, the chaplain repeatedly urged her to make a full confession but, even as the noose was placed around her neck, she called out, "I am innocent as a lamb."

In September 1848, a fifty-six-year-old labourer, Richard Geering, died of a suspected heart attack in Guestling near Hastings. He left behind a widow, Mary Ann, to whom he had been married for thirty years; and five children, three of whom – James George and Benjamin – still lived in the family home.

Three months after his father's death, when twenty-one-year-old George became ravenously hungry after a series of bouts of vomiting, he was treated by Dr Pocock, who struggled to find the cause of his illness. George died on 27th December, and, although Dr Pocock did not know what had killed him, he recorded that his death was due to natural causes. In March 1849, twenty-six-year-old James also died after suffering similar symptoms; and, again, Dr Pocock saw nothing untoward. When, though, within a month, twenty-year-old Benjamin began vomiting and complaining of excessive hunger, he was attended by the more observant Dr Ticehurst, who immediately suspected foul play.

Ticehurst insisted on altering the content and administration of Benjamin's diet; and, when his mother was no longer preparing his food, he quickly began to recover. As this confirmed the doctor's suspicions about the deaths of his father and brothers, he recommended that the coroner order their exhumations. Although the bodies were in various states of decomposition, the stomachs and intestines were remarkably well-preserved. Richard's and James' organs were found to contain arsenic, and, while none was detected in George's gut, it was noticeably inflamed.

Inquests were held in a tavern and, as Mary Ann, was named as the obvious suspect, she was charged with murder despite having no apparent motive for the crimes. It was erroneously reported that she hoped to gain money from the burial club but, as several newspapers pointed out, the sum she would receive was so paltry that it would not have been worth her while. It was suggested, too, that she had simply grown tired of Richard and wanted him dead, but this did not account for the murder of her sons.

Benjamin testified against her during her trial, and his evidence was sufficient to convince the jury of her guilt. On the evening before her execution, she confessed that she had poisoned them all, but failed to give any explanation for why she had done it.

Many guilty women went to their deaths protesting their innocence in the hope of obtaining a last-minute reprieve, but in 1849 and 1851, two women were hanged, one of whom was as much a victim as a criminal; and one of whom was probably innocent.

In 1821, Rebecca Small, a market-gardener's daughter, married a labourer, Philip Smith, who spent most of his meagre income on drink. When drunk he repeatedly abused his wife and it was probably against her will that, over three decades, she bore him ten children. Their pitiful financial situation might have been eased when Rebecca's father died leaving her one hundred pounds[y] but Philip squandered the whole amount and, by the time of the birth of their youngest child, Richard, in 1849, the family was virtually destitute.

Rebecca, 'an inoffensive and industrious woman', was drained, ill and exhausted and, although Richard was a healthy baby, she repeatedly sighed to her neighbours that he was dying. The neighbours were even more disconcerted when she asked them to help her buy arsenic, and, when Richard died soon afterwards, they reported their suspicions to the coroner. A post-mortem revealed that the baby had been poisoned, and Rebecca was arrested and charged with his murder.

While awaiting trial in Devizes, she not only admitted killing Richard but also confessed to poisoning eight of her other children by letting them suck arsenic from her finger. When the horrified prison chaplain asked what had possessed her to behave so fiendishly, she replied that she wanted to save them from destitution. By the time that Richard was born, she added, she was convinced that

---

[y] Approximately £12,000 in today's values.

she was dying and she dreaded the thought of leaving him with his brutal father.

Crowds from miles around turned out to watch her sad execution, which took place in Devizes on 23rd August – the last time that a woman was hanged in Britain for infanticide.

Although Rebecca's story was tragic, there is no doubt that she had killed her children, but the same could not be said for Sarah Chesham, who was executed for murder two years later.

In 1845, Sarah had been married for eighteen years and, having given birth to six children, she supplemented her labourer husband's wages by taking in washing; tending the sick; and assisting expectant mothers during their confinements. Until then, her life had been quite unremarkable but, thanks to the introduction of the Reinsch Test, it was about to move in a new and terrifying direction.

As investigators were now able to prove the presence of poison, stories of murders, which would have previously gone undetected, regularly appeared in the press. This led to suspicion about every unexpected illness, and completely innocent people found themselves accused of murder. So it was that, when two of Sarah's sons, James and Joseph, died of cholera, gossips claimed that they had been poisoned by their mother.

The rumours eventually died down and Sarah continued to assist new mothers and women in childbirth until one young woman, Lydia Taylor, accused her of poisoning her baby, Solomon, who she said had been healthy until she fed him a bow of rice that Sarah had prepared. The story spread so quickly that Sarah was nicknamed 'Sally arsenic', and a magistrate ordered the exhumations of James and John. When Professor Alfred Swaine Taylor detected arsenic in both boys' remains, Sarah was arrested.

Tittle-tattle reached epidemic proportions as neighbours rushed to give evidence. Some said they had heard Sarah warning her other children that, if they did not behave, they would go the same way as their brothers. A family dog was said to have died at the time that James and John fell ill; and other children complained of pains in their stomachs.

None of this proved that Sarah had administered or even possessed poison; and the only person in the village known to do so was baby Solomon's father, Thomas Newport. Refusing to accept that Sarah might be innocent, the gossips twisted this revelation to suggest that she and Newport were accomplices. When Solomon died, no traces of arsenic were found in his body, but this did not alter the villagers' belief that Sarah had killed him; and, as the inquest jury comprised only local people, she was named as being responsible for his murder.

Unsurprisingly, when she appeared at the Essex Assizes, an impartial judge dismissed the case for lack of evidence. To the chagrin of her neighbours, Sarah was free to return to the village, but there was nothing she could do to stem the gossip.

In 1850, when her husband, Richard, died of consumption, Professor Swaine Taylor discovered a very small quantity of arsenic in his remains. He concluded that Sarah must have been plying him with small doses of poison; and, when her home was searched, arsenic was discovered in a bag of rice. The problem facing the judiciary was that there was no doubt that Richard Chesham had died of consumption and so it would not be possible to charge his widow with murder. Instead, therefore, they opted for attempted poisoning – a charge which also potentially carried a death sentence.

Alone and friendless at her trial at the Chelmsford Spring Assizes, Sarah had to listen as her former friends gave evidence against her. One woman, Hannah Philips, claimed that she had told the prisoner of her own unhappy marriage, to which the prisoner replied that unwanted husbands could be disposed of with arsenic. Even if this uncorroborated story were true, it did not prove that Sarah had poisoned Richard, but the jury took it as fact and found her guilty.

When the judge, Mr Justice Campbell, put on his black cap, he was so overcome with emotion that several minutes passed before he was able to sentence Sarah to death. The publicity that the verdict received led to such widespread panic at the thought that wives could slowly poison their husbands that, when the new Arsenic Regulation Bill was debated in the House of Lords, the Earl of Carlisle demanded that it included an amendment, prohibiting the sale of poisons to women and children.

Sarah was hanged in Chelmsford Gaol on 25th March 1851, but, even after her death, her reputation continued to be maligned. Three years later, 'Sally arsenic' remained such a reviled figure that one M.P. told the House of Commons that: 'Sarah Chesham...committed fourteen murders by poisoning, and...never showed any symptoms of repentance or of fear."[69]

In 2019, however, barristers Jeremy Dein and Sasha Wass reviewed the evidence for the BBC series *Murder, Mystery & My Family*. When they presented their findings to the retired judge, David Radford, he ruled that the conviction was unsafe as it was 'affected by prejudice and unfounded allegations.' At the time of writing, Sarah's descendants are seeking a posthumous pardon.

# Chapter 15 – The Greatest Criminal Who Ever Lived

While Sarah Chesham was awaiting execution, twenty-nine-year-old Catherine Wilson was busily working her way up the social ladder. Having begun life as a lowly maid, she had ascended to the position of housekeeper for a retired sea captain, Peter Mawer, to whom she made herself so indispensable that, within two years, he made her the chief beneficiary of his will. The timing of his decision could have been more fortuitous for Catherine, as, a short time later, he died in excruciating pain. The doctor, perplexed by his symptoms, could only conclude that the captain must have unintentionally overdosed on prescribed medicines.

Her employment terminated, Catherine collected her inheritance and set off for London, where she took up with a man named James Dixon, whom she passed off as her brother. In the autumn of 1855, they found lodgings in Bedford Square in the home of a widow, Maria Soames but, by Christmas, Catherine had run out of money, and was reduced to pawning her watch and other personal items. Mrs Soames, however, was reasonably wealthy and, when Catherine learned that she was also about to receive a substantial legacy, she made a greater effort to ingratiate herself with the landlady.

James Dixon, meanwhile, was becoming a hindrance to Catherine's ambition when, and, in June 1856, he became seriously ill with vomiting and diarrhoea. Catherine told the doctor that her 'brother' was in the habit of treating his rheumatism and gout with colchicum – a highly toxic extract of the Autumn Crocus plant, which was occasionally used in the treatment of auto-immune diseases. The doctor warned her of the risks of taking colchicum without strict medical supervision, to which she replied that she was well aware of the danger. When James

Dixon died a few days later, the doctor recommended a post-mortem, but Catherine refused, with the usual excuse that her brother had always had a horror of being cut up after his death.

A few weeks later, Mrs Soames went on holiday and, on her return, Catherine told her that thieves had broken into the house and taken many of her valuable pieces of silver. Distressed as she was, Mrs Soames had no reason to doubt Catherine's story, particularly when she claimed that some of her own belongings had also been stolen.

Over the next few months, Catherine's financial fortunes continued to decline but she had a solution in mind, which she put into effect in mid-October. Mrs Soames suffered a bilious attack, which her doctor, George Whidborne, believed had been caused by something she had eaten, despite her insistence that she had only eaten a fresh pork pie. Catherine, however, told a neighbour that the landlady had confessed to taking poison.

When Mrs Soames died on 18th October, her brother, who had seen her looking hale and hearty only a few days earlier, was so astonished that he urged Dr Whidborne to arrange a post-mortem. The doctor willingly obliged but, to his surprise, nothing suspicious was discovered, and so death was recorded as due to natural causes.

Boosted by her success in having escaped detection, Catherine seized her chance to make money from the landlady's demise. She presented Mrs Soames' daughters with an 'IOU' ostensibly from their mother, to whom, she said, she had loaned ten pounds some weeks earlier. Once the unsuspecting daughters had repaid the debt, Catherine left Bedford Square and disappeared.

Three years later, she resurfaced in Lincolnshire at the home of Mrs Jackson, an acquaintance who died suddenly soon after Catherine's arrival. Within a few months she struck again – her victim being James Dixon's aunt, Ann Atkinson.

Mrs Atkinson was visiting Catherine at her new home in Lambeth when her husband received a telegram saying that his wife was seriously ill. He hurried from his Cumberland home but, by the time that he reached London, Ann had died – leaving Catherine an IOU.

The ease with which she had killed her victims and obtained money from their bereaved relations was making Catherine complacent when, in 1862, she made a fatal mistake that would be her undoing. As she had once made herself indispensable to the sea captain, Peter Mawer, she now ingratiated herself with a widow, Sarah Carnell, with whom she found employment as a nurse and companion. Like the captain, Mrs Carnell became so dependent on her faithful attendant that she altered her will in her favour; but, of course, Catherine was so eager to receive her inheritance, that she prepared to hasten her employer's demise. This time, however, rather than using colchicum, she opted for vitriol – sulphuric acid.

As Mrs Carnell lay in bed, Catherine handed her a glass of warm water, urging her to drink it down as 'it will warm you.' Unsurprisingly, as soon as the corrosive touched her tongue, Mrs Carnell spat it out, burning a hole in the blankets. Catherine panicked and fled but the police soon found her and, when they charged her with attempted murder, she calmly explained that the incident with the vitriol had been an unfortunate accident. She had gone to the pharmacy, she said, to buy a soothing draft for Mrs Carnell but the chemist was absent, and the assistant who served her must have accidentally mixed up the bottles and given her vitriol by mistake.

The story was presented at her trial but, in his summing up of the case, the judge, Baron Bramwell, pointed out that, if the glass bottle had contained vitriol, it would have become so hot that it would have exploded before she arrived home. Nonetheless, to the surprise of the court and the press, the jury believed Catherine's account and found her not guilty.

> "An expression of delight," wrote her barrister, "came upon the face of the woman, whose appearance, by-the-bye, was a very peculiar one, her chin being the most receding one I have ever seen. She turned round abruptly to leave the dock, but the instant her foot was on the floor of the Court, she was [re-]arrested."[70]

While she had been awaiting trial, the friends of her previous victims had voiced their suspicions to the police, with the result that, unbeknown to her, seven bodies had been exhumed. Although some were too decayed to provide any evidence, sufficient colchicum was found in Mrs Soames' remains to warrant Catherine's arrest for murder.

Ironically, if she had been found guilty of the attempted murder of Sarah Carnell, she might have served a lengthy sentence and then been released. Now, charged with murder, she appeared before Mr Justice Byles in the Old Bailey, anticipating an appointment with the hangman. In his summing up, the judge warned that, if she were acquitted, no living person could sit down safely to a meal; and when he had sentenced her to hang, he privately told her barrister, "I may tell you that in my opinion you have today defended the greatest criminal that ever lived."[71]

He had not, however, yet heard of Mary Ann Cotton, to whom murder came as easily as breathing.

Money was scarce, life was harsh and pit disasters were regular occurrences in the Sunderland mining village of Low Moorsley, where Mary Ann Robson was raised. When she was ten years old, her father was killed in a pit accident, leaving her mother to raise the family in virtual destitution. The future was unappealing for the ten-year-old girl, who knew that she was expected to follow the same path of drudgery that her mother and all the other miners' wives had followed, but she dreamed of a better life, far from the coal dust and the dreariness of the harsh routine; and, from an early age, she was determined to turn her dream into reality.

At the age of twenty in 1852, she married a local miner, William Mowbray, but, more desperate than ever to improve her lot, she urged him to take a job with a railway company four hundred miles away in Cornwall. It must have come as a great disappointment to discover that life in Cornwall was no better than life on the Durham coalfields. Living in spartan conditions in a makeshift railway settlement, money was always scarce and Mary Ann was continuously pregnant, giving birth to five children, all but one of whom died in quick succession.

Eventually, she and William returned to Sunderland with their surviving daughter, Isabella, but tragedy appeared to have followed them. The remarkably fecund Mary Ann continued to produce children at a rapid rate but, equally rapidly, one after another, they succumbed to 'gastric fever'. To make matters worse, an accident left William unable to work, and, with no wages coming into the household, Mary Ann was again faced with destitution. She grudgingly nursed her husband until he died of gastric fever, leaving her to find consolation in the arms of a lover, Joseph Nattrass; and the thirty-five pounds that she received from the Prudential Life Insurance Company.

With no husband to support her, Mary Ann needed to earn a living, and so, leaving Isabella in the care of her mother and stepfather, she took a job as an untrained nurse in the Sunderland Infirmary. She cared for her patients so tenderly that one of them, George Ward, married her as soon as he was discharged from hospital. After only fourteen months, he, too, died of gastric fever, leaving his widow his possessions and a pay-out from a life insurance company.

Within two months, Mary Ann found her next victim when she read an advertisement in the paper from James Robinson, a recently-widowed shipwright, who was seeking a housekeeper to care for his motherless children. When Mary Ann presented her credentials as a former nurse, she appeared to be the ideal candidate and in November 1866, she moved into Mr Robinson's home, just a few weeks before the unexpected death of his baby son.

A few weeks later, on receiving word that her mother was seriously ill, she hastened to Seaham Harbour, where she helped herself to the sick woman's possessions while she was dying of...gastric fever. With her mother gone, Mary Ann took her daughter, Isabella, back to the Robinsons' home but, within a short time, the little girl died, as did two more of James Robinson's children.

Employing all her guile and charm, Mary Ann consoled the grieving father, and, when she told him that she was pregnant, he felt duty-bound to marry her. Alarmed and suspicious, his sisters urged him not to trust her but he ignored their warnings and the wedding took place in August 1867. Three months later, Mary Ann gave birth to a daughter, who died soon afterwards; and, by the time that a son, George, was born the following year, James Robinson realised that he ought to have listened to his sisters.

While Mary Ann was repeatedly pressing him to take out a life insurance policy, he discovered that she had been drawing on his accounts, accruing debts and failing to bank the money that he had asked her to deposit. Seeing that she had only married him for his money, he threw her out of the house, undoubtedly saving his own life, and that of the baby, George.

Having nowhere else to go, Mary Ann sought help from a childhood friend, Margaret Cotton, who had left her employment to care for the two sons of her widowed brother, Frederick. A single father, Mary Ann surmised, must be in need of a wife but, as Margaret Cotton stood in the way of her plans, there was no option but to dispose of her in the usual fashion.

Six months after Margaret's death, Mary Ann, pregnant again, married Frederick Cotton, without disclosing the fact that she was still legally married to James Robinson. Her latest marriage of convenience did not prevent her from resuming her affair with Joseph Nattrass, and, when she grew tired of Frederick, he, too, succumbed to gastric fever. Their baby died soon afterwards, as did one of Frederick's sons, and so, despite having had so many children, Mary Ann was left with only stepson, Charles.

After Frederick's death, Nattrass moved in with Mary Ann, but, predictably, he too, died a few months later, and she decided that it was time to rid herself of Charles Cotton. Surprisingly, instead of poisoning him as she had so many others, she took him to the workhouse and told the overseer, Thomas Riley, that he was preventing her from finding work, and she did not see why she should keep him when he was not her child. Taken aback by her callousness, Riley replied that he could not take the boy for such a flimsy reason, at which Mary Ann shrugged and said that it did not really matter because Charles was such a sickly child that he would soon 'go the way of all the Cottons'.

Less than a week later, when Riley heard that the boy was dead, he was so disconcerted that he warned the doctor not to sign the death certificate until the police had carried out an investigation. Dr Kilburn performed a post-mortem but, finding nothing untoward, concluded that Charles had died of natural causes. Fortunately, the doctor's assistant was more conscientious and carried out his own more thorough tests on the innards. When he detected the presence of arsenic, Mary Ann was arrested, and the remains of several of her other victims were exhumed and sent to Thomas Scattergood in Leeds for analysis.

Although Scattergood found arsenic in the remains of some of the bodies, Mary Ann stood trial only for the murder of Charles Cotton. Her defence claimed that there was no proof that she had administered the poison, but, when the prosecution produced witnesses who had seen her purchase arsenic, the jury had no doubt that she was guilty.

On the eve of her execution, she reputedly told the chaplain that, although she had poisoned Charles, it was not intentional. She said nothing about her many other victims. The following morning, 24th March 1873, she was hanged in Durham Gaol by William Calcraft.

Murder had come so easily to Mary Ann Cotton that, by the time that she poisoned her stepson, it was almost an addiction – an addiction which she shared with Elizabeth Berry, who was likewise so devoid of humanity that she calmly killed her husband, her mother and even her own children.

Twice-married Elizabeth had first been widowed when her soldier husband was killed in the Afghan Wars, leaving her to care for their little daughter, Edith. Being an attractive woman, she soon remarried and gave birth to a son, but both he and his father died unexpectedly soon afterwards.

Having trained as a nurse, Elizabeth found a position in the Oldham Workhouse Infirmary, leaving little Edith in the care of her sister-in-law. Like Mary Ann Cotton, she insured her daughter's life for ten pounds, and took out an additional joint policy, whereby she or Edith would receive one hundred pounds if the other predeceased them.

Shortly after Christmas 1886, she invited Edith to stay with her at the Oldham Workhouse. Inmates and employees commented on the little girl's cheery disposition and healthy appearance but, on New Year's Day, she began vomiting violently. Elizabeth gave her a milky drink and asked the workhouse surgeon, Dr Patterson, for something to calm her stomach, and, as a result, she began to recover.

The following day, when her symptoms returned, Elizabeth showed the doctor a towel covered in Edith's bloody vomit, from which emanated a strange acidic smell. While making up a prescription for the child, Dr Patterson noticed that a bottle of medical creosote[z] was missing from the dispensary, but, at that time, he thought no more about it. On examining Edith, however, he was so alarmed by an inflammation in her mouth that he sought a second opinion from a colleague, who agreed that it appeared as though the child had swallowed a corrosive. When she died two days later, Dr Patterson refused to sign the death certificate until he had performed a post-mortem.

The autopsy showed that Edith had ingested sulphuric acid, and, when this was revealed at the inquest, the jury returned a verdict of wilful murder against her mother. This naturally gave rise to suspicions about the deaths of her husband and son, and more recently, that of her mother, Mary Ann Finlay. The coroner deemed that the husband and son had died so long ago that there was little point in examining their remains, but he ordered the exhumation of Mrs Finlay's body, which was found to contain a substantial amount of poison.

After sitting through a four-day hearing in St George's Hall, Liverpool, the jury took less than an hour to find Elizabeth guilty of murder. In passing the death sentence, the judge, Mr Justice Hawkins, described the murder as cold-blooded, merciless and cruel and he had no doubt that the jury had reached the right verdict. Pending

---

[z] Medical creosote was used as an antiemetic and in the treatment of tuberculosis, as well as an antiseptic

execution, she was detained in Walton Gaol, where she played the part of pious woman, whom God had afflicted with suffering. In a sentimental letter to the Oldham Poor Law Guardians, she begged them to place a flower from her on Edith's grave, and added that she gladly submitted herself to the will of God, who alone knew the agonies that she endured. 'I think I must have loved my dear ones amiss,' she concluded, 'since God, either in His mercy or His jealousy, has removed them.'

If she hoped that this might win her a reprieve, she was to be disappointed. On a bitterly cold morning in March 1887, the hangman, James Berry, entered her cell and Elizabeth immediately recognised him as a dancing partner during a policeman's ball in Manchester some years earlier. Berry acknowledged that he, too, remembered the dance, but this did not prevent him from carrying out his duties which resulted in Elizabeth being the first of only two women ever to be hanged in Walton Gaol.

# Chapter 16 – Fatal Attractions

No one could have suspected that Christiana Edmunds was anything but a respectable middle-aged woman, living quietly with her mother and sister in Brighton. Although she was later described as 'vain, silly, and obviously weak-minded'[72], she appeared to be the archetypical Victorian spinster: devoid of passion, a little bitter but otherwise thoroughly 'decent.'

Beneath that pious veneer, however, forty-three-year-old Christiana harboured a secret obsession. She was madly in love with a married physician, Dr Beard, who, with a measure of restraint, briefly returned her affection. He soon regretted his momentary lapse as he loved his wife, Emily, and had no intention of breaking his marriage vows to satisfy the whims of his adoring patient.

Christiana, unwilling to accept his rejection, convinced herself that, if it were not for Emily, she and the doctor would have a wonderful life together. With that end in mind, she visited the Beards and gave Emily a box of chocolates, which made her so sick that her husband guessed that she had been poisoned and ordered Christiana never to visit again.

Far from being deterred, Christiana formed a bizarre plan to make the doctor believe that someone else had poisoned the chocolates. She sent random children to Mr Maynard's confectionery shop, with instructions to purchase specific chocolates, which she injected with strychnine, before returning them to the shop with the excuse that she had made the wrong selection. Mr Maynard then innocently sold them to other customers, unaware that they were the cause of a sudden surge of sickness in the district.

The situation became more serious when a four-year-old boy, Sidney Barker, who was holidaying in

Brighton, died after eating some chocolates that his uncle had bought for him. Mr Maynard was arrested and charged with murder, and, when he stood trial, Christiana brazenly gave evidence against him. Fortunately, the jury found him not guilty and he, having been acquitted, destroyed all the chocolates in his shop.

Christiana duly resumed her practice of lacing confectionary and cakes with poison, this time using arsenic in place of strychnine. As an added precaution, she took a train to London from where she posted several contaminated packages to prominent citizens in Brighton, including one to her own address, to divert suspicion from herself.

The police, continuing their investigations into Sidney Barker's death, placed a notice in the Brighton papers, offering a reward for any information leading to the arrest of the poisoner. On reading this, Dr Beard immediately thought of Christiana, and when he told the police what he knew of her, her writing was compared to the writing on the poisoned packages and she was arrested.

Her trial opened in August 1871, but, as her barrister argued that it was impossible to select an impartial jury in Brighton, she was transferred to Newgate in London. Five months later, she appeared at the Old Bailey, where the most telling evidence against her came from the chemist who had sold her strychnine. Her barrister saw that her only defence was a plea of insanity – a condition that ran in her family – but the usually-lenient judge, Baron Martin, pointed out that, although she was 'weak minded', she knew what she was doing and was, therefore, responsible for her actions.

Several doctors, who attended the hearing, agreed.

"There [were]," the British Medical Journal reported, "...no symptoms of insanity prior or subsequent to the act, which, be it observed, was not an act done in a moment, but a series of acts spread over many months, and indicating considerable deliberation and forethought. We are not surprised that this plea of insanity was rejected by the jury."[73]

When the jury found her guilty and the judge pronounced the death sentence, Christiana bizarrely claimed that she was pregnant. A medical examination proved that this was not the case and, for the first time she realised the perilousness of her situation. She became so distraught that the prison surgeon gave her a sedative, sincerely hoping 'that she would find in him not only a great healer of the body, but a tender and compassionate physician to her poor aching mind.'[74]

As ever, there were petitions for a reprieve on the grounds that insanity ran in the family; her brother was in an institute for 'idiots' and her father had been insane. Surprisingly, in view of his comments at the trial, the judge asked the Home Secretary to arrange further psychiatric assessments. Christiana was examined for over four hours by Sir William Gull – who had recently treated the Prince of Wales for typhoid – and Dr Orange, the Deputy Medical Superintendent of Broadmoor Criminal Lunatic Asylum. Both were convinced that she was insane, and as a result of their testimony, her sentence was commuted to detention in Broadmoor.

For the next thirty-five years, Christiana remained incarcerated, never once expressing remorse for her crimes. Her doctors concurred that she was 'feeble minded' and was prone to long periods of depression followed by periods of hyperactivity – which was widely referred to at that time as 'circular insanity.' She was flirtatious, too, and developed an obsession with her appearance, which confirmed the medical opinion that she was suffering from 'moral mania.'

"She did not occupy herself about things of interest in the asylum," wrote a psychiatrist, "and used to do such childish acts as collect dust from the bricks of her cell to redden her lips and cheeks."[75]

As she aged, she became calmer but continued to display the classic signs of 'mental enfeeblement', and, when she died at the age of seventy-eight in September 1907, the doctor recorded her death was due to 'senile decay.'

A family history of insanity might suggest that Christiana was *non compos mentis,* but even the most rational people can adopt extreme behaviour when in the grip of passion. Mary Ann Britland was a perfectly reasonable wife and mother until she developed an obsession with a married neighbour, Thomas Dixon, who worked with her in a factory in Ashton-under-Lyme.

Privately, she schemed and dreamed of the life that they would have together; and that image was so sacred to her that, when her nineteen-year-old daughter, Elizabeth, discovered her obsession, she saw no alternative but to ply her with Harrison's Vermin Killer – a lethal concoction of arsenic and strychnine.

In the middle of the night, on 8th March 1886, Elizabeth awoke, seized with vomiting, diarrhoea and uncontrollable twitching. Her symptoms persisted throughout the whole of the next day, and when she died at eight o'clock that evening, her body stiffed very quickly, which was a sign of strychnine poisoning. An inattentive doctor, however, put her death down to natural causes, which inspired in Mary Ann the confidence to dispose of her husband by the same method. Again, the doctor mistook the strychnine-induced muscle spasms for an epileptic fit and, for the second time in two months, Mary Ann Britland got away with murder.

Being a kindly neighbour, Thomas Dixon's wife, Mary, pitied the poor widow, grieving the loss of her husband so soon after the death of her daughter. No one, said Mary, should have to be alone at such a sad time, and so she invited Mary Ann to stay with her, unaware that the object of her pity was already planning to kill her.

On May 13th, less than a fortnight after the death of Thomas Britland, Thomas Dixon had to spend the night away from home, and, when he returned early the next morning, he found his wife gasping for breath and twitching uncontrollably. He sent for the doctor, who saw the similarity between Mary's symptoms and those of Thomas and Elizabeth Britland, but there was nothing he could do and, within an hour, Mary Dixon was dead.

Neighbours were convinced that Mary Ann had murdered the unfortunate woman; and, when the doctor heard that she had anxiously discussed the effects and detection of poisons, he informed a magistrate, who ordered the exhumation of the three bodies. As arsenic and strychnine were found in the remains, the magistrate mistakenly believed that Mary Ann Britland and Thomas Dixon had been having an affair and had conspired to kill Dixon's wife so that they could be together. Both were arrested but, while Mary Ann immediately confessed to murder, the horrified Thomas vehemently denied the accusation and, as there was no evidence that he had ever shown the slightest interest in Mary Ann, he was released without charge.

Throughout her trial, Mary Ann repeatedly expressed sincere remorse but this did not prevent the jury from finding her guilty of the murder of Mary Dixon. In a desperate panic, Mary Ann cried out, begging for mercy so persistently that the judge could hardly pronounce the death sentence. When he finally managed to utter the fateful words, she screamed in terror and her cries could still be heard in the courtroom long after she had been taken down to the cells.

For the next three weeks in Strangeways Prison, she constantly wept, sang hymns and begged for forgiveness until she was but a 'haggard wreck of her former self.' Relatives visiting her, shortly before her execution, asked her to confess that she had also murdered Thomas and Elizabeth, and, although she did not reply, she hung her head in shame.

"When the morning of the execution came," wrote the hangman, "she was so weakened as to be utterly unable to support herself, and she had to be practically carried to the scaffold by two female warders. For an hour before the time of the execution she had been moaning and crying most dismally, and when I entered her cell she commenced to shriek and call aloud. All the way to the scaffold her cries were heart-rending, though her voice was weak through suffering, and as the white cap was placed over her head she uttered cries which one of the reporters described as 'such as one might expect at the actual separation of body and spirit through mortal terror.' The female warders held her on the drop until the noose was fixed, then their places were taken by two male warders who stepped quickly back at a signal which I gave them, and before she had time to sway sideways or to collapse the drop fell and the wretched woman was dead."[76]

Reporters who witnessed the execution were shaken by the 'painful scene' and could only take comfort from Berry's adroitness that ensured that she died instantly.

Four years later, James Berry was again called upon to execute a woman who had become the victim not only of her obsession with a married man but also, perhaps, her own insanity.

John Pearcey had been only one of the many lovers of Mary Wheeler, but, although they were never married, she used his name for the rest of her life. When their affair was over, she was never short of male company for, despite not being conventionally pretty, she had sufficient charm to beguile several wealthy men, one of whom paid the rent on her rooms in London's Kentish Town. In spite of the financial benefits of being a kept woman, Mary found so little joy in her lifestyle that she drowned her depression in drink, and attempted suicide on three separate occasions.

In 1888, her spirits lifted when a removal man, Frank Hogg, appeared in her life and made a greater impression upon her than any of her previous lovers had done. Mary was well aware that Frank was simultaneously seeing another woman, Phoebe Styles, who soon announced that she was pregnant with Frank's child. Desperate to avoid responsibility, Frank considered emigrating but Mary, terrified of losing him, persuaded him to stay and marry Phoebe.

Marriage did not prevent him from continuing to see Mary – a situation which his docile wife graciously accepted. In the months that followed, the women became friends, and when Phoebe gave birth to a daughter, Mary became a second mother to her. For eighteen months these amicable arrangements continued but, beneath the façade, Phoebe grew to dislike and fear her rival, while Mary resented the wife who stood between her and Frank. Their simmering enmity remained in check until the autumn of 1894 when Phoebe made a comment which Mary found so offensive that her repressed anger exploded, bringing their relationship to a violent conclusion.

On 24th October, Mary invited Phoebe for tea, and she arrived in the mid-afternoon, pushing the baby in a large pram. At about four o'clock, neighbours heard screaming and the shattering of crockery but, as the blinds were drawn, they could not see what was happening. In the darkened room, Phoebe had made an offhand remark that so ignited Mary's fury that she seized a poker and smashed her skull.

Faced with the problem of disposing of the body, she unsuccessfully attempted decapitation before forcing it into the pram on top of the baby. She then set off through the darkness, intending to dump the gory cargo as far from home as was possible but, when she reached Hampstead, the pram collapsed and Phoebe's body rolled onto the street. Leaving it corpse where it lay, Mary hurried on with the baby in the broken pram until she realised that the child, too, was dead, having suffocated under the weight of her dead mother. Leaving the dead baby and the pram in Finchley, she returned home, having completed a circuitous six-mile trek, and began to clean up the blood.

By the time that Mary was safely back in her lodgings, Phoebe's body had been found but the only clue to her identity were her initials stitched into her undergarments. While the public panicked that the half-decapitated woman was a victim of Jack the Ripper, the police placed a notice in the morning papers, hoping someone would come forwards who recognised the stitched 'P.H.'. The next morning, Frank's sister, Clara, who was already concerned that Phoebe had not returned home the previous evening, saw the article and feared that she might be the dead woman. Ironically, she asked Mary to accompany her to the morgue to identify the body. Clara immediately recognised the deceased as her sister-in-law but Mary pulled her away insisting that she was mistaken. Moreover, when Clara mentioned that Phoebe was last seen on her way to Mary's house, she claimed that she had never arrived.

Alerted by her suspicious behaviour, Inspector Banister questioned Mary's neighbours, who reported having seen her pushing a large pram during the previous night. When his officers searched her home, Mary sat playing the piano, singing and whistling loudly to drown out their questions. Bloodstains and splatters were visible across the floor and walls; a bloody knife was found in the kitchen; and, when asked to explain the bloodstains on her clothing, Mary shrieking, 'Killing mice! Killing mice!' and played the piano more loudly.

A month after the murder, Mary stood on trial at the Old Bailey where her barrister was prevented from entering a plea of insanity by her insistence that she was innocent. Consequently, in view of the number of witnesses and the mass of circumstantial evidence, a guilty verdict was virtually inevitable. Before passing sentence, when the judge asked if she there were any reason why she should not be hanged – the euphemistic form of asking if she were pregnant – she replied, 'Only that I am innocent of the charge.'

While in Newgate Prison, awaiting execution, she impressed the chaplain and the wardresses by her tractability and apparent resignation to her fate. She was unaware that her defence team was busily preparing a petition to the Home Secretary in the hope of gaining a reprieve on the grounds of insanity. Drawing attention to her previous suicide attempts, they also noted that she had been prone to fits and hallucinations, and appeared to have no recollection of the crime. Further, they added, although she had killed Phoebe Hogg, there was no evidence of premeditation, and, if she struck out in a moment of anger, the charge should at least be reduced to manslaughter.

The press, too, took up her cause, suggesting that she had no motive for murder, as, if she had wished to marry Frank Hogg, she would not have persuaded him to marry Phoebe Styles. The Home Secretary, Henry Matthews, however, saw no reason to grant a reprieve and the execution date was set for 23rd December.

On the evening of the 22nd, Mary made a strange request to her solicitor. She asked him to place a notice in a leading Spanish newspaper: 'M.E.C.P. Last Request M.E.W. Have not betrayed.' For the rest of the night she was guarded by three wardresses, who were surprised by the calmness with which she prepared for death. Impressed, too, was the executioner, James Berry, who arrived the following morning to lead her to the scaffold.

"When introduced to her I said, 'Good morning, Madam,' and she shook my proffered hand without any trace of emotion. She was certainly the most composed person in the whole party. Sir James Whitehead, the Sheriff of the County of London, asked her if she wished to make any statement, as her last opportunity for doing so was fast approaching, and after a moment's pause she said: 'My sentence is a just one, but a good deal of the evidence against me was false.' As the procession was formed and one of the female warders stepped to each side of the prisoner, she turned to them with a considerate desire to save them the pain of the death scene, and said, 'You have no need to assist me, I can walk by myself.' One of the women said that she did not mind, but was ready and willing to accompany Mrs Pearcey, who answered, 'Oh, well, if you don't mind going with me, I am pleased.' She then kissed them all and quietly proceeded to her painless death."[77]

The solicitor duly placed the notice in the Spanish paper although he had no idea of what it signified. M.E.W. are the initials of her maiden name: Mary Eleanor Wheeler; but, as 'M.E.C.P.' has never been identified, the purpose of the message and its intended recipient remain a mystery.

# Chapter 17 – Strangers in the House

By the middle of the nineteenth century, almost one-and-a-half million women worked as domestic servants in Britain, making service the most common form of female employment. The advantages were obvious for orphans or girls from very poor families, as it could mean an escape from an overcrowded hovel, with a guarantee of an income, regular meals and a bed to sleep in – albeit a bed that was sometimes shared with other servants or even an employer. Adversely, though, the hours were long and the work was physically demanding, and, until 1860, employers were legally entitled to beat their servants if they deemed them insolent or lazy.

"It is the custom of Society to abuse its servants," wrote Isabella Beeton. "…Matronly ladies, and ladies just entering on their probation in that honoured and honourable state…talk of servants, and, as we are told, wax eloquent over the greatest plague in life while taking a quiet cup of tea…It is another conviction of Society that the race of good servants has died out, at least in England…that there is neither honesty, conscientiousness, nor the careful and industrious habits which distinguished the servants of our grandmothers and great-grandmothers; that domestics no longer know their place."[78]

Mrs Beeton, the doyenne of household management, believed that mistresses and maids could only live happily together if they were prepared to acknowledge their mutual dependence.

"With a proper amount of care," she wrote, "in choosing servants, and treating them like reasonable beings, and making slight excuses for the shortcoming of human nature, they will, save in some exceptional case, be tolerably well served, and, in most instances, surround themselves with attached domestics."[79]

The 'exceptional cases' were capable of inspiring terror into the middle and upper classes, for, no matter how good a reference might be, there was no guarantee that an apparently devoted retainer would not steal from, or, worse, threaten the life of an employer. Even the Royal Family was not immune to the danger, as Queen Victoria's uncle, the Duke of Cumberland, learned to his cost. While the Duke was sleeping, his valet, Joseph Sellis, crept into his room and attacked him so violently with a sword that his brain was visible through the deep gash in his head, and only the hangings from his four-poster bed saved him from a fatal injury. When the alarm was raised, Sellis fled, locked himself in his room and slit his own throat.

If a man in the Duke's position could be so viciously assaulted, what hope was there for a diminutive widow who shared her home and her bed with a malevolent young woman whom she had trustingly employed as a companion and maid?

Sixty-one-year-old Elizabeth Mundell could hardly be described as wealthy, as she lived in a rented room with only one bed in a house in Brewer's Green in Westminster. Nonetheless, she managed to pay for the services of a maid, Martha Browning, who had only been with her for a few weeks when she noticed that Mrs Mundell kept a five-pound note in a sewing case beneath her mattress. For the sake of the five-pound note, Martha was willing to kill, and, on 1st December 1845, she tied a cord around Mrs Mundell's neck while she was sleeping.

The older woman woke with a start and desperately cried out, 'Murder! Murder!' which brought a neighbour, Mrs Cheshire, hurrying to find out what was happening. The door was locked from the inside and there was no response to her knocking until, eventually, Martha called that there was nothing to worry about, and Mrs Cheshire returned to bed.

A short time later, she was woken again when Martha came to her door to tell her that Mrs Mundell was very poorly. Mrs Cheshire sent her to fetch the old lady's daughter, Ann Glaze, who lived with her soldier husband, Edward, just around the corner in Rochester Row.

Martha reached the Glazes' house shortly before eight o'clock, and told Ann that her mother had had a fit. They raced back to Brewer's Green and, when they saw Mrs Mundell lying on the floor with a cord around her neck, Martha ran from the room, telling all and sundry that her poor employer had hanged herself.

The inquest concluded that Elizabeth Mundell had indeed committed suicide but neither Ann nor Edward was convinced by the verdict. While clearing his mother-in-law's room, Edward noticed that the five-pound note was missing; and the underside of the mattress was wet with urine, suggesting that Elizabeth had died in bed and the mattress had then been turned over. Edward came to the conclusion that the maid had killed her mistress and then placed her body on the floor to create the semblance of suicide.

Determined to entrap her, Ann casually asked Martha if she could lend her some money, as the funeral expenses and doctor's fees had left her short of cash. Martha replied that she had some savings, which she had left in the care of a former employer, but, once she had retrieved them, she could lend Ann one pound. Convinced that the savings did not exist, Ann and Edward said that they would accompany her to the supposed employers' home, but when they reached the vicinity of the house, Martha insisted on going on alone. She returned soon afterwards with a five-pound note, which Edward offered to change in a nearby pub, but Martha refused to allow him to take it and said she would change it herself. She went into the pub and came out moments later, complaining that her employer had deceived her as the five-pound note was not legal tender.

Ann had known all along that her mother's note was just an advertising gimmick for the sewing company. In place of the standard 'Bank of England', it read, 'Bank of Elegance' and was never intended to be used as legal tender.

Rather than accusing Martha outright, Ann suggested that they should all return to the home of the former employer to ask him why he had deceived her. At this, Martha panicked, claiming firstly that she needed the toilet and then that she was too ill to walk any further. Edward replied that, unless she accompanied him back to her employer's house, he would have to fetch a policeman, which so alarmed her that she broke down completely and confessed to having killed Elizabeth Mundell.

Edward held her until a passer-by had found a policeman, who arrested her on the spot and escorted her to the nearest station. There, in a state of near-collapse, she was charged with murder. In the hours that followed, she became still more distressed and, during the initial hearing, she cried and sobbed so loudly that, several times, the magistrate was forced to halt the proceedings. Nonetheless, he deemed that she was fit to stand trial and, by the time that she appeared in the Crown Court, she had regained sufficient composure to remain stoically silent when the judge pronounced the death sentence.

A relatively small crowd gathered outside Newgate to watch the execution, and, as one journalist noted, it comprised very few females but mostly men of 'the lower orders.' Although she walked calmly to the scaffold, a Member of Parliament, arguing for the abolition of capital punishment, erroneously claimed that she 'she fell down insensible; in that state she was executed.'

It is possible that the Member of Parliament had confused her with Sarah Thomas, who was hanged in Bristol for a similar crime, three years later.

Unlike Mrs Mundell, Miss Elizabeth Jefferies of Bristol was such a vindictive employer that she found it very difficult to find or retain reliable housemaids. Those who entered her service were given only meagre meals; they were not permitted to sit by the fire; and, if they annoyed her, she fiercely threatened to beat them. Unsurprisingly, few stayed with her for more than a couple of weeks, but, in late January 1849, she engaged seventeen-year-old Sarah Thomas who was far less malleable than her predecessors.

In the early hours of 3rd March, a neighbour was awoken by screams coming from Miss Jefferies' house, but, as the noise soon faded, she went back to sleep and thought no more about it. The following morning, Sarah Thomas appeared on her doorstep to tell her not to be alarmed about the previous night's commotion as it was nothing but a cat screeching.

Soon afterwards, another neighbour saw Sarah and a male accomplice carrying parcels from the house; and, that afternoon, when Miss Jefferies' friend visited, she was surprised to find the shutters drawn and no one at home. By then, Sarah had returned to her parents' house in the 'lawless' suburb of Horfield, bringing with her a quantity of silver and jewellery.

Four days passed before the neighbours alerted the police to Miss Jefferies' disappearance, and, when officers broke into the house, they found her lying on a blood-soaked bed with a fatal wound to her head. Her little dog had also been killed and stuffed into a privy; and, when Inspector Bell examined the scene, he found matted grey hair and blood on a stone that Miss Jefferies used as a doorstop.

Naturally, Sarah became the prime suspect and, when witnesses reported having seen her going in the direction of Horfield, Inspector Bell and Sergeant Carp made their way to her parents' house. Her mother, Ann, kept them waiting on the doorstep, claiming that Sarah was not at home, but, when they eventually gained admission, they found her hiding in a coal hole, surrounded by Miss Jefferies' possessions. Further pieces of the dead woman's silverware were discovered around the house, with the result that both Sarah and her mother were arrested.

In custody, the allegedly 'simple-minded' Sarah was sufficiently imaginative to invent a tale to explain how she came by her employer's possessions. A former maid, Maria Lewis or Maria Williams, she said, had returned to ask Miss Jefferies for a reference and, when she refused to provide one, Maria was so angry that she said she would kill 'the old duchess.' Although Sarah maintained that she had played no part in the murder, she confessed that she had agreed to say nothing about it in return for a share of the dead woman's belongings.

While the police went in search of a maid named Maria Lewis or Maria Williams, a little girl, Mary Sullivan, came forwards with an entirely different tale. She had, she said, seen two riflemen entering the house and had watched while one of them murdered Miss Jefferies. The police wasted more time investigating this claim before learning that the child was 'a feeble-minded epileptic', who enjoyed inventing stories.

Having failed to find any record of Maria Lewis or Maria Williams, Inspector Bell interviewed Sarah's predecessor, Lucy Chadd. She confirmed that Miss Jefferies had been a most disagreeable employer, but she had a strong alibi, being in Bath at the time of the murder.

When all other lines of inquiry had failed to produce any credible suspects, Sarah was indicted for murder and sent for trial at the Gloucester Assizes.

Although she was facing a capital sentence, she laughed throughout the proceedings, until the judge donned his black cap, at which point she screamed hysterically before collapsing.

Her execution on 19th April 1849, was one of the most distressing hangings ever witnessed in the city. Sarah, screaming and struggling, had to be dragged up the two flights of stairs of the gallows, where she continued to shriek and writhe so desperately that the prison governor was overcome with emotion and fainted. Eventually, William Calcraft had to throw her over his shoulder to carry her up the ladder to the scaffold.

A seasoned journalist, Ebenezer Austin, described the event as the most disturbing execution that he had witnessed.

> "The time having arrived for the culprit to ascend the drop," he wrote, "those outside the gaol were startled by the screams that proceeded from within its precincts. At last we saw the condemned girl being literally carried up to the scaffold, struggling and shrieking for her life, and with a brother reporter who accompanied me I turned away. Returning after such an interval as assured us that the dread sentence of the law had been carried into effect, we found the multitude still gazing at the suspended body of the wretched girl, having had the last extremity of human suffering demonstrated to them. But there was no solemnity; ribald jests were bandied about; and, after waiting to see the corpse cut down, the crowd dispersed, and the harvest of the taverns in the neighbourhood commenced."[80]

Fortunately, this was the last public hanging in Bristol.

Apart from the crowds who attended the executions, the public took little interest in the murders of Elizabeth

Mundell and Elizabeth Jefferies, but, in 1872, when Marie Caroline Besant Riel was killed by her cook, the nation was gripped by every detail of the crime and subsequent trial.

What caught the public attention was the apparent exoticism of the victim. Madame Besant Riel, a French actress, lived in Park Lane – one of the most exclusive streets in London – and moved in the highest social circles as the mistress of the seventy-two-year-old Earl of Lucan. In reality, she was neither as exotic nor as wealthy as the newspaper readers imagined, for, although her neighbours were aristocrats, she could only afford one housemaid, Eliza Watts, and a Belgian cook, Marguerite Dixblanc, who spoke very little English.

According to Eliza Watts, Madame Besant Riel was a bad-tempered employer, who constantly found fault with the Belgian cook. Rather than being cowed by her criticism, Marguerite responded with equal ferocity and passion, although Eliza did not know exactly what was said, as their fiery arguments were always in French.

On Sunday 7th April 1872, Madame Besant Riel called into the kitchen on her way out for a walk. Seeing that Marguerite had not yet started to prepare dinner, she seized a saucepan from her hand and placed it over the fire. Marguerite retaliated by demanding her wages, saying that, since her work was so unsatisfactory, she would find employment elsewhere; but Madame Besant Riel laughed mockingly, remarking that the only other work she would find was walking the street. The insult so incensed Marguerite that she seized Madame Besant Riel by the throat and choked her to death.

In a desperate effort to conceal the body, she tried unsuccessfully to force it into the water-closet and then into the dustbin before tying a cord around the neck intending to drag it upstairs. At that moment, Eliza returned from an errand but the cook, denying her access to the kitchen, sent her out again to buy some beer. When she had gone,

Marguerite forced the body into the pantry and locked the door before hurrying around the house to snatch valuable items and jewels from the safe in order to fund her escape.

When Eliza returned with the beer, the two women ate lunch together as though nothing had happened, but when Madame Besant Riel had not returned home by the mid-afternoon, Eliza began to worry. Marguerite reassured her that 'madame' had gone to stay with friends; and, at four o'clock, she announced that she was going to church. Instead, she picked up her bag of loot and caught the boat train to Paris, where some acquaintances, Monsieur and Madame Bouillon, allowed her to stay in their home in return for some of the stolen items.

Back in England, Eliza Watts waited up until after midnight, wondering why both women had disappeared It came as a relief to her the next morning when Madame Besant Riel's daughter, Julie, returned from a holiday in France. When Eliza told her that her mother was missing, Julie sent her to find a policeman, and, during her absence, she searched the house, finding the body in the pantry.

Although it did not take long for the police to trace Marguerite to Paris, their efforts to bring her to trial were delayed by the need to liaise with the French authorities. Ironically, if she had fled to her native Belgium, she could have escaped justice as no extradition treaty existed between Belgium and Britain; but, since such a treaty existed between Britain and France, as soon as the official papers had been signed, a French detective arrested her. After a further delay as discussions took place regarding the possible arrest of the Bouillons, two British policemen, Pay and Druscovitch, escorted her back to England.

The delay had served only to heighten the public's interest in the story and, by the time that the prisoner arrived in Dover, large crowds had gathered to catch a glimpse of the murderess. From Dover, she was taken by train to London, and by cab to Newgate Prison to await her trial in the Old Bailey.

Her barrister saw little point in denying that she had killed her employer but he argued that she had acted under provocation. Moreover, he stated that, due to her language difficulties, she could not have a fair trial as she was unable to follow all the proceedings and to instruct him accordingly. In his summing up, the judge, Baron Channell acknowledged that Marguerite had 'laboured under the disadvantage of being a foreigner' but he reminded the jury that, no matter what words Madame Besant Riel used to goad her, unless she felt her life was in danger, there was no excuse for murder. The jury found her guilty but recommended mercy on the grounds of provocation and lack of premeditation. Channell agreed and, as he pronounced the statutory death sentence, he assured Marguerite that he would take the jury's recommendation to the appropriate authority.

The Home Secretary commuted the sentence to life imprisonment and, in the years that followed, Marguerite repeatedly petitioned for a reprieve. In 1893, after serving twenty years in Knaphall Prison in Surrey, she finally walked free.

Much of the public's sympathy with Marguerite Dixblanc was based on the knowledge that Madame Besant Riel had been such a harsh employer; but when Kate Webster used the same excuse for murdering Julia Thomas, she met only with disgust and outrage.

Mrs Thomas, a fifty-four-year-old widow and former teacher, was decidedly eccentric in her habits, often indulging in her love of travel without telling anyone where she was going. Nonetheless, she was intelligent and well-educated, which makes her decision to employ an Irish maid, Kate Webster, in January 1879, all the more surprising. Had she bothered to ask for references or looked into Kate's career, she would have learned that she had history of petty crime and had recently served twelve months in Wandsworth Prison for theft.

Kate was so delighted by her 'very comfortable' position with the 'nice old lady' that she saw no need to put any effort into her duties. She became so lackadaisical that Mrs Thomas was forced to upbraid her for her carelessness, and took to inspecting the rooms that she had cleaned to ensure that they had been done properly. Tensions mounted in the household until, at the end of February, Mrs Thomas gave the maid notice of dismissal. Kate later claimed that leaving was a mutual decision, but this seems unlikely since she had no other employment and, when the date of her departure arrived, she pleaded to be allowed to stay a few more days until she had found somewhere to stay and a new position.

On Sunday 2nd March, Mrs Thomas went to church as usual, and, although she had given Kate the afternoon off, she expected her to be back before she returned to church for the evening service. Kate, however, went to the pub and came back much later than agreed, which led to another argument, leaving Mrs Thomas very shaken and agitated. She attended the service but left earlier than usual, and, on returning home, went straight upstairs to tell Kate that she must leave.

Fuelled, perhaps, by her afternoon's drinking, Kate flew into such a rage that she hurled Mrs Thomas down the stairs before seizing her by the throat and strangling her. By her own account, she then lost control of her senses, and was so determined to avoid arrest that she disposed of the body by chopping it into pieces. Using a razor and a meat-saw, she cut off the head, dismembered the torso and opened the stomach to pull out the entrails, which she threw into the fire. The flesh was boiled in a copper cauldron, which she offered to some local urchins as pork dripping!

"I was bewildered, and acted as if I was, mad," she later confessed, "and I did everything I could possibly to conceal the occurrence and keep it quiet, and everything regular, fearing the neighbours might suspect that anything had happened. I was greatly overcome both from the horrible sight before me and the smell, and I failed several times in strength and determination, but was helped on by the devil in this vile purpose."

Throughout the night, she chopped, boiled and scrubbed away the blood, before putting all the remains except the head into a wooden box. At one point, needing a break, she visited her friends, the Porters, taking the head with her in a bag and leaving it under the table while they drank together.

As Mrs Thomas had regularly gone on her travels without informing her neighbours, no one was concerned by her disappearance. Consequently, if Kate had followed Marguerite Dixblanc's example, she could have vanished long before anyone realised that a murder had been committed. Instead, determined to profit from her crime, she called herself 'Mrs Thomas' and began selling off her late employer's property.

She told her friends, the Porters, that she had received a legacy from a relative, and asked their help to sell some of the items that she had inherited. Among them were Mrs Thomas false teeth; and a large wooden box, which, she claimed, she needed to take to Richmond Bridge to meet a gentleman who wished to purchase its contents. The Porters' son, Robert, helped her to carry it and, when they reached the bridge, Kate told him to go home as she no longer needed his assistance. As he left, he heard a loud splash as though something heavy had been thrown into the river.

The following day, a workman found the box washed up on the bank, and was horrified to discover that it contained a gruesome array of body parts. Without a head, the police were unable to identify the victim but they placed a full description of the find in the morning papers, leaving Robert in no doubt that this was the box that he and Kate had carried.

Meanwhile Kate, still assuming her late employer's name, made contact with a second-hand dealer, John Church, with a view to selling some of Mrs Thomas' clothes and furniture. He accompanied her to the house and began removing some chairs but, when a neighbour, Mrs Ivy, saw what was happening, she told Kate to stop the sale at once.

Church, having heard Mrs Ivy's complaints, suspected that Kate had been using a false identity. He searched through the items that she had sold him and, finding a letter addressed to Mrs Thomas in a dress pocket, he worked out a way to test his suspicions. He visited the letter's sender and asked him for a description of the intended recipient, who clearly bore no resemblance to the woman using her name. When he discussed his discovery with the Porters, they agreed that the only course of action was to tell the police.

When the police arrived at Mrs Thomas' house, they found plenty of evidence of the horror that had occurred: blood-stains everywhere; charred remains in the fire grate and lumps of fat behind a boiler. The suspect, however, unnerved by Mrs Ivy's interference, had fled, but the police rightly presumed that she would have returned to her native Ireland, and, when they contacted their Irish counterparts, Kate was arrested.

During her trial at the Old Bailey, her barrister presented a compelling defence, pointing out that there was no means of identifying the remains in the box, and, even if they were those of Mrs Thomas, she could have died of natural causes. His efforts failed to impress the jury, and Kate was found guilty of wilful murder.

The evening before her execution in Wandsworth Prison, she made a full confession, which was printed in the following day's papers.

"For anything I have done," she concluded, "which I now declare before God to be as I have stated, I implore His mercy, and I heartily forgive those who have been so ready to condemn me of the actual murder, which I declare in this my dying confession to be as I have stated. The public mind, my solicitor informs me, was greatly biased against me; and all the harsh and untrue remarks passed upon me in the height of peril and trouble I freely from my heart forgive. I do not complain of the fairness of my trial, nor have I any complaint to make, against anybody other than as I have now confessed. I thank the judge who tried me, for the fairness he showed, and his readiness to have me fairly dealt with and I now pray Almighty God to have mercy on me in the last moments of my mortal existence. I have been foolishly led away to my ruin by those who should have protected me, and may my miseries, troubles, trials, and awful fate serve as a warning to young girls never to be led away from the path of virtue and honesty...I am perfectly resigned to my fate, and am full of confidence in a happy eternity. I die with great fortitude and confidence in my faith and in our blessed Lord, whom I beseech to have mercy on my soul."

At her request, a Catholic priest visited the execution cell and, once he had given her absolution, she calmly slept until five o'clock in the morning. When the governor and priest arrived, she thanked them for their kindness and with firm steps accompanied them to the scaffold. A brief cheer resounded from the crowd outside the prison when the flag was raised to signify that the sentence had been carried out.

A curious postscript to this story occurred in 2011. Builders, working on an extension to the home of the naturalist and television presenter, David Attenborough, discovered a skull in the back garden. Attenborough's house is close to the now demolished home of Mrs Thomas, and a pub that Kate Webster regularly frequented. Forensic analysis confirmed that the skull was that of the murdered woman, which Kate had, at some point, either buried or simply discarded.

# Chapter 18 – Partners in Crime

There can surely have been few lonelier experiences than that of a murderess, living with guilt and the terrible fear of arrest and execution, while unable to unburden herself to any other living being. To have a partner in crime might, at least, alleviate the stress and loneliness, but it also brought the added fear of being betrayed. Sharing so dreadful a secret could, at first, bring a couple closer together, but, when faced with a death sentence, partner often turned against partner in a desperate attempt to avoid the noose.

In the early 1840s, Swiss-born Maria de Roux found a comfortable position as lady's maid to the wife of a Member of Parliament, Lady Palk, with whom she made regular excursions on the Great Western Railway. In the course of these trips, she became friendly with a railway guard, Frederick Manning, and, in spite of her extensive duties, she found time to pursue a romance.

When, in 1846, Lady Palk died, Maria found a new position as lady's maid to Lady Blantyre, a daughter of the Duchess of Sutherland, Mistress of Robes to Queen Victoria. As much of her time was spent at the Blantyres' London home, Stafford House, she saw Fred less frequently than had been her wont, although he occasionally visited.

It was only a matter of time before Fred had a rival: an Irish petty thief, Patrick O'Connor, whom Maria met while accompanying Lady Balantyre on one of her many continental tours. Although he was twenty years her senior, he wasted no time in pursuing her, nor she in responding to his advances. They met on the boat on the way to Boulogne and immediately began their affair while the other passengers were sleeping. From then onwards, O'Connor regularly visited Maria in London, and enjoyed bragging to his friends about his connections to a Swiss woman who lived in Stafford House.

In 1847, when Manning heard that he had a rival for Maria's affections, he was so fearful of losing her that he proposed. To strengthen his suit, he told her that he was about to come into a substantial legacy, which might or might not have persuaded her to accept his offer. Following the wedding and a honeymoon in Devon, the new Mrs Manning travelled to Switzerland with Lady Blantyre before resigning from her service.

Fred's inheritance failed to materialise; and, soon after the wedding, he was dismissed from the railway company. Fortunately, though, Maria had received a generous gift from Lady Blantyre, which, when combined with the savings that she and Fred had accrued, enabled them to purchase The White Hart Inn, in Taunton. In spite of their mutual infidelities, the couple lived contentedly together and for a while business was good, but everything changed dramatically when two of Fred's friends, who had been staying in the White Hart, were arrested for their part in a train robbery.

From then onwards, locals, suspecting that Fred had either been involved in the robbery or had betrayed his friends to the police, avoided the inn and, as the takings dwindled, the Mannings were forced to leave Taunton for London. There, they took on a new pub but again the business failed and so they settled in Bermondsey where Maria was forced to earn a meagre living as a dressmaker.

This was not the life of which she had dreamed while serving as a lady's maid in some of the finest houses in the country. Now, she was in such reduced circumstances that she and Fred were forced to sell of most of their possession, keeping only the furniture. The only prospect of a more secure future came from O'Connor, who had made Maria a beneficiary of his will; and, as neither Fred nor Maria was prepared to wait for him to die a natural death, they embarked on a murderous plan.

Their neighbours knew that O'Connor was a regular visitor to their Bermondsey home, and they had no doubt that he and Maria were lovers. What astounded them was Fred's complicity in this arrangement as the two men were often seen together in the garden late at night, smoking and laughing amicably. The neighbours gossiped, too, about the Mannings' strange activities, as all through the night 'there was nearly always a light burning; and there always appeared to be something mysterious going on.' Moreover, Fred had several disconcerting conversations with a number of lodgers, regarding the uses of chloroform and other sedatives; and shopkeepers noticed that he had purchased a large crowbar, of the kind used to raise flagstones; and Maria had bought quicklime and a shovel.

By late summer 1849, the Mannings were ready to put their plan into action; and, on the 8th August, Maria invited O'Connor to dinner. Frustratingly, he arrived with a companion, forcing Fred and Maria to postpone their plan until the following evening. Although it is impossible to know exactly what happened the night of 9th August, subsequent investigations outlined the most likely scenario. O'Connor was lying on his side when the first blow was struck, suggesting that Fred had soaked his tobacco in laudanum to subdue him. A post-mortem revealed that his skull was smashed by several blows to the side of his head, after which he was stabbed with a chisel and shot with a pistol.

> "All the wounds on his head which were sufficient to cause death…were at the right side; and the bullet, which may have been fired at him to finish the work begun with the blunt cutting instrument wherewith these fractures were effected, was found over the right eye, as if driven through the head from the rear. That this was the case, and that the projectile in question was propelled by an insufficient power, is obvious from the fact that the

bullet lodged in the skin over the right eye. This would lead in some sort to the conclusion that it was fired from a badly-loaded air-gun, or with a small charge of gun-cotton from a common pistol or other fire-arm. The course of this wound, however, shows that it was not fatal; and, therefore, the murder must have been consummated with a heavy hammer or some similar instrument, for the back part of the skull was found entirely beaten in fragments into the brain by the violence of successive blows."[81]

His body was forced into a hole beneath a flagstone in the kitchen, and quicklime was poured over him to accelerate decomposition. Exhausted after completing so gruelling and gruesome a task, Maria waited until the next morning to scour O'Connor's lodgings for valuables. Not content with her pickings, she returned the following day to gather some share certificates and a few other valuable items.

By then, O'Connor's work colleagues were concerned about his absence and made inquiries into his last known movements. During a search of his lodgings, they discovered that his shares and cash were missing, and learned that Maria had not only visited the house twice since his disappearance, but also that she had invited him to dinner on the last day that he had been seen alive.

When they reported their findings to the police, an officer went to Bermondsey to question Maria, who coolly stated that O'Connor and his friend had visited on 8th August but that was the last time that she had seen him. As he failed to appear on the 9th, she said, covering all her tracks, she feared he was ill and had been twice to his lodgings to see if he was alright, but he was not at home on either occasion.

Beneath her calm exterior, Maria was terrified that the police would search the house and the body would be discovered. As soon as the officer left, she decided to flee with O'Connor's cash and shares, abandoning Fred in the process. When Fred came in, she told him that they needed to move house, and so he must go out and sell the furniture. During his absence, she hurried to the station and caught a train to Edinburgh. When Fred returned and realised that she had deceived him, he, too, fled, making his way to Jersey.

Unbeknown to the Mannings, the police had been keeping a watch on the house and, when they saw Maria leaving with her luggage, they were soon on her trail. Seeing that she was heading for Scotland, they telegraphed the Edinburgh police to keep a look out for her, and, in the meantime, they began a thorough search of the house in Bermondsey. An observant officer noticed that the edges of two of the kitchen flagstones were damp as though they had been recently scrubbed; and when, with the help of a colleague, he lifted them up, he found O'Connor's naked body.

Within a week, the Scottish police arrested Maria as she attempted to sell some of O'Connor's shares.

"It is absolutely ridiculous to suggest that I murdered Mr O'Connor," she told the arresting officers. "He was the kindest friend I had in the world. If he has been murdered, it was done by that villain of a husband of mine, while I was out for a walk. I hope you gentlemen will catch him."[82]

Before she was sent back to London, Scottish law required her to appear at the Edinburgh Police Court, where again she maintained her composure as she insisted that she was innocent.

"She walked into the dock with a firm, unfaltering step;" wrote one eye-witness, "and, during the whole time she was at the bar, her countenance did not betoken the slightest symptom of agitation or alarm....She was very neatly dressed; and, from her easy and graceful manner, she evidently a person who has mixed a good deal in society. She is not, however, by any means what may be styled beautiful...There is a kind of dogged expression about her face, which...led not a few of the on-lookers to say that she was just such a woman as could assist in the devising and carrying out such a deed as that in which, she implicated."[83]

Within a fortnight, Fred was also arrested and taken back to London so that the couple could stand trial together in the Old Bailey. The widely-reported case aroused such interest that several foreign ambassadors joined peers and aristocrats in the public gallery. In spite of the evidence against them, both pleaded not guilty, and Maria's barrister, William Ballantine, attempted to use a loop-hole in the law to have her acquitted. As a wife was expected to obey her husband, Maria could not be found guilty if, *after* Fred had killed O'Connor, he told her to help him to dispose of the body and conceal the crime. If, however, she assisted him in the planning and execution of the murder, she would been as a co-conspirator and the rule would not apply. It was vital, then, for Ballantine to show that Maria had no advanced knowledge of Fred's plans, and that she was not at home when he murdered O'Connor.

Fred, likewise, attempted to put all the blame onto Maria, claiming that he had played no part in either the murder nor the concealment of the body. The jury, however, believed that a woman would not have sufficient strength to inflict so many violent injuries or to lift the flagstone and force the body into the hole.

Ultimately, both were found guilty and sentenced to hang but, whereas Fred silently resigned himself to his fate, Maria claimed her right to address the court.

"There is no justice nor fair treatment for a foreign subject in this country," she railed. "I have had no proper protection from the judges, or from the prosecutor, or from my husband. I am wrongly condemned…I think that I am not being treated like a Christian, but like a wild beast of the forest. The judge and jury will have it on their consciences for giving a verdict against me. I am not guilty. I have lived in respectable families, and can produce testimonials of character. If my villain of a husband, through jealousy and revenge, chose to murder poor Mr. O'Connor, I really don't see why I should be punished."[84]

Ballantine's valiant attempts to obtain a reprieve were all in vain, and, on the morning of her execution, Maria fruitlessly tried to kill herself by cutting her throat with her finger nails. Ballantine conceded defeat, later admitting that, 'I defended her unsuccessfully, as she was hanged; and, although she was my client, I suspect she was the power that really effected the deed.'[85]

Charles Dickens witnessed the hangings and was so appalled by the 'ribald' and obscene behaviour of the drunken crowds that he wrote to *The Times* to express his disgust at the 'fightings, faintings, whistlings…brutal jokes, tumultuous demonstrations of indecent delight when swooning women were dragged out of the crowd by the police, with their dresses disordered.'[86]

In spite of his indignation, however, Dickens found in Maria Manning the inspiration for Madame Hortense, the 'powerful high and passionate' French lady's maid in *Bleak House,* who commits murder and attempts to frame her mistress for the crime.

If Members of Parliament hoped that the publicity surrounding the Mannings' execution would deter other potential partners-in-crime, they were soon to be disillusioned. Only five months later, Elias Lucas and Mary Reeder conspired to murder a totally innocent woman.

Twenty-five-year-old Elias had been married for four years to Susan Reeder, when, in the winter of 1849, he began an affair with her younger sister, twenty-year-old Mary, who worked with him on a farm in Cambridgeshire. As their relationship intensified, Mary left her job and moved in with her lover, ostensibly to care for her sister during her imminent confinement. The baby was born in February 1850, but lived for only for a short time, and a few days later, Susan also fell ill.

A neighbour, Mrs Potter, happened to visit and, seeing Susan retching and vomiting, was shocked that neither Elias nor Mary had sent for a doctor. Taking that responsibility on herself, Mrs Potter described Susan's symptoms to the local physician, who initially suspected that she was suffering from puerperal fever – a common and often fatal hazard of childbirth at the time. In view of the seriousness of the condition, the doctor set out at once but, by the time he reached the Reeders' home, Susan was dead.

Within a few hours, her father came to view the body and was so disconcerted by her pained expression and the stiffness of her limbs that he asked the doctor to perform a post-mortem. The stomach and intestines were sent to Professor Swaine Taylor, who confirmed that she had been poisoned by arsenic.

In response to the police inquiries, Elias' employer stated that he had given him a sachet of arsenic to kill weeds on the farm; and, when questioned, Elias turned on his lover, admitting that he had taken the poison home, as Mary had asked him to bring it to treat her chilblains. Under pressure, he also confessed that he and Mary had been having an affair, but he denied any involvement in Susan's death and asserted that it had never occurred to him that Mary had murderous intentions.

The couple were tried together at the Cambridge Assizes, where the prosecution made much of their failure to call a doctor; and Elias' alleged comment that Susan's death freed him to marry Mary. When the judge, Mr Wightman, sentenced them to death, Elias refused to acknowledge his guilt but, while awaiting execution, Mary made a full confession, admitting that they had planned the murder together.

In front of a crowd of about forty-thousand people, the couple stood together at the scaffold with their heads bowed as in prayer.

"I am going to God!" Elias cried as Calcraft pulled the lever to open the trap door and, at that moment, the crowd surged forwards so quickly that several women were trampled and seriously injured.

One indignant journalist, who witnessed the executions, was more concerned about the behaviour of the prisoners than the unruliness of the spectators. Like all condemned prisoners, Mary and Elias had been given the sacraments, and this had inspired in Elias such enthusiasm for eternal salvation that he had gone to his death in good spirits like an early Christian martyr. Quick to remind his readers that the condemned man was an adulterer and a murderer, the journalist was so appalled that he had died filled with hope of heaven rather than the fear of damnation, that he recommended denying the sacraments to all capital prisoners in the future!

The formation of unholy alliances was not confined to married couples or lovers. Siblings also conspired to kill, and their victims were often members of their own family. Sarah and Abigail Stubbs, for example, had a reputation for sullenness and were known to treat their parents most cruelly. In their Harrogate home, their mother, Ann, earned a living by taking in washing, and, in July 1848, she offered the daughters a shilling each to help her. When the work was completed, the sisters demanded more than the agreed payment and, when Ann refused to give it to them, they became so aggressive that she called on her husband to throw them and all their belongings out of the house. The sisters ferociously leaped upon her and, when their father intervened, a passer-by heard Mrs Stubbs cry, 'They will kill us! I am going to fetch the police!'

Refusing to leave the house, the girls set off upstairs and, when their father followed them, they kicked and pushed him down to his death. During the inquest at the Commercial Inn, the coroner deemed there was insufficient evidence to prove wilful murder, as Mr Stubbs might have slipped and fallen. Sarah and Abigail Stubbs walked free, and their father's demise was recorded as death by misadventure.

There were no such doubts in the case of two Irish sisters, whose crimes were so notorious that they became known as 'The Black Widows' or 'The Borgias of Liverpool.'

In 1880, a fifty-year-old widow, Catherine ('Catty') Flannagan, and her younger sister, Margaret, took a house in Skirving Street in the Walton area of the city in the hope of making a living by taking in lodgers. Catty's son, John, a healthy young man in his early twenties, moved in with them; and they soon took in four paying guests: Thomas Higgins, a widowed builder, and his eight-year-old daughter, Mary; and Patrick Jennings and his sixteen-year-old daughter, Margaret.

Not content with the lodgers' rents, the sisters developed the more lucrative scheme of investing in several burial clubs, which would enable them to profit from the death of any member of the household. Of course, they had no intention of waiting for someone to die, and, as a test run for their other victims, they poisoned Catty's son with arsenic obtained from fly papers. The scheme worked to perfection, as the physician, Dr Hill, certified that the young man had died of bronchitis, and the burial club paid out quickly without asking any questions. Two days after his death, John was hastily buried in the Ford Roman Catholic Cemetery, and the sisters made a reasonable profit from his demise.

Forty-three-year-old Margaret, meanwhile, had set her sights on Thomas Higgins, and, in October 1882, after a brief romance, they were married. Within months of the wedding, his little daughter, Mary, died suddenly, and, once again, the burial clubs paid out to the sisters' advantage. Only two months passed before Margaret Jennings followed her to the grave, which set neighbours' tongues wagging about the succession of unexpected deaths in the household.

To escape the gossip, Catty, Margaret and Thomas moved across the city to Latimer Street in Kirkdale but, as their income declined, they were forced to downgrade to basement lodgings in neighbouring Ascot Street. Disgruntled about their failing financial fortunes, the sisters conspired to make Thomas Higgins their next victim; and, this time, not content with the prospect of pay-outs from five separate burial clubs, they also took out a number of life insurance policies.

In September 1883, Thomas died after suffering from griping pains in his stomach, leading the doctor to certify dysentery as the cause of death. The sisters confidently prepared to collect the payments from the burial clubs and insurers but they had failed to consider the reaction of Thomas' family. His brother, who had seen him only a few days earlier, could not believe that so healthy a man had died of natural causes; and he became even more alarmed when he learned that Thomas had a life insurance policy. He made further inquiries, and, on discovering how many policies had been taken out on his brother's life, he contacted the police.

On the day of Thomas' funeral, the sisters drowned their sorrows in alcohol and, the more they drank, the more argumentative they became. A neighbour overheard Margaret accuse Catty of poisoning her husband, to which Catty replied:

"He wasn't your husband. He was your fancy-man, and an old Orangeman[aa]."

The day was already descending into chaos when the police arrived with orders from the coroner to halt the funeral so that a post-mortem could be performed. Fearing that her crimes were about to be discovered, Catty fled, leaving Margaret to face the consequences alone. A search of the house produced various sachets and bottles of poison, including one found in Margaret's pocket; and, when the post-mortem revealed that Thomas had died of arsenic poisoning, Margaret was arrested and the coroner ordered the exhumations of other possible victims.

Catty evaded the police for only a week before she was arrested, at which point she made a remarkable statement to her solicitor. She and Margaret, she said, had not acted alone but were part of a wider conspiracy involving at least four other women who were responsible for multiple deaths across Liverpool. She was willing, she said, to testify against her co-conspirators in returned for immunity from prosecution or a reduced sentence. The police investigated her allegations and believed she was telling the truth, but, due to a lack of evidence, the Director of Public Prosecutions, Sir John Blossett Maule, refused her offer to testify, and ordered that she and Margaret should stand trial for the murder of Thomas Higgins.

Predictably, both were found guilty and, on 3rd March 1884, Bartholomew Binns hanged them in Kirkdale Prison. They were fortunate in that they both died instantly, despite the hangman's reputation for drunkenness and botched executions. A week after the death of 'the Black Widows', Binns returned to Kirkdale Prison to hang Michael McLean, who had murdered a Spanish sailor.

[aa] An Orangeman is a member of the Irish Protestant Orange Order.

Despite the governor's protests that he was too drunk to carry out his duties, Binns refused all assistance and, consequently, the prisoner was left dangling from the rope for over fifteen minutes. Unsurprisingly, Binns was immediately dismissed.

A more unlikely lethal partnership was that of Susannah Garnett and her eldest daughter, Elizabeth, who were charged with starving Elizabeth's young sister to death. In fairness, they appear to have acted more through ignorance than malice as they and the rest of their family were desperately undernourished. Mr Garnett, a shepherd who was often absent and frequently ill, earned such a pittance that Mrs Garnett and her daughters stitched shirts and other garments to bring in a few extra pennies. If the girls failed to complete their work, they were deprived of food, with the result that, at the time of the crime, one sixteen-year-old daughter weighed only just over three stones[bb].

Amazingly, the sixteen-year-old survived but her younger sister was already chronically malnourished when she became too ill to finish stitching lace onto a pillow. As usual, she was deprived of food for two days and two nights, and, according to her sisters, her last words were, 'Oh Lord Jesus, help me to do my work next week.'[87]

When she died, Susannah and Elizabeth were arrested for her murder but, by the time that their case came to trial, this was reduced to manslaughter. Apathetic and vacant, they appeared unconcerned when they were found guilty and sentenced to four years penal servitude. Confinement in Millbank Prison was far more luxurious than the life to which they had become accustomed. They ate well and, as they began to put on weight, both became more animated than they had been when arrested.

---

[bb] Forty-six pounds or twenty-one kilograms

"In contradistinction to the slowness, almost torpidity, of her earlier days," the prison matron reported, "the younger Garnett began to exhibit a briskness over her work, and an interest in it, significant of contentment with her position. The famine-haunted look about her keen grey eyes had by this time wholly disappeared. The mother, too, made rapid progress to some semblance of healthy womanhood, and both worked diligently on towards a better position."[88]

They showed no interest, though, in the other prisoners, and, when the wardresses took pity on them and arranged for them to be together, it was apparent that they cared little for one another.

Neither spoke about the crime nor expressed any regret for what had happened, but, one day, a wardress noticed that Susannah appeared preoccupied, and asked her if she were fretting about the length of her sentence.

"I've nothing to fret about, lady," she replied. "I'm better off here than I ever was…We were all starving there together, and my husband…was very ill, and my daughters were weak too, and we had nothing to give them – nothing at all to give them or ourselves, and so my daughter died. But, lady, it wasn't in our power to help her."[89]

Unsurprisingly, when they had completed their sentences, neither was relieved to be released from prison.

Coincidentally, in the same year that the Garnetts were arrested, another woman named Garnett was starved to death by her husband. William Garnett could not use the excuse that he lacked the means to provide for his wife, as he earned a reasonable living but he kept it all for himself. Often, he returned home for work with joints of meat that his wife, Martha, was expected to cook for his dinner, but neither she nor their children were allowed to share it. Martha was so desperate that she regularly begged help from her neighbours, and, even as she was dying of consumption, William failed to help her. When she died, an inquest was held in the Clerkenwell Workhouse, where the doctor stated that death had been hastened by starvation, and, as a result, William Garnett was charged with manslaughter.

# Chapter 19 – Van Diemen's Land

Prior to the construction of the vast Victorian prisons, transportation was a convenient means of punishing convicts for whom the death penalty was deemed too extreme. Not only did it solve the problem of where to house offenders when the town lock-ups and castle cellars were full or no longer fit for purpose, but also it provided the government with an ideal means of establishing colonies. Originally transportees were sent to the Americas but, following the War of Independence, they were taken instead to Van Diemen's Land[cc] or New South Wales, where they were expected to marry and raise children to create a strong British presence in Australia.

From the prisoners' point of view, transportation was obviously preferable to hanging but it could hardly be described as a lenient sentence. The voyage itself was perilous and many prisoners died before reaching their destination, either from disease or through maritime disasters. In 1833, for example, when the female convict ship, *Amphitrite*, ran aground off Boulogne, the captain refused French offers of help for fear that, once his prisoners reached land, they would make a break for freedom. The women remained locked in the bowels of the ship, with the result that over a hundred-and-thirty convicts and several crewmen drowned. Two years later, over two hundred Irish women and children suffered the same fate when the convict ship, *Neva*, hit a reef and sank off the coast of Tasmania.

Even when the voyage was relatively calm, life aboard a convict ship was far from comfortable. A boatswain, Owens, who survived the sinking of the *Amphitrite*, gave evidence that:

---

[cc] Tasmania

"The language and behaviour of some of the women, was outrageous and disgusting beyond anything the men had ever heard. Owens has frequently been obliged to throw pails of water over them, as the only means of keeping them at a distance from the crew. All this language and behaviour the children were exposed to hear and see night and day...The doctor had the sole management of them...There was no attempt at restraint, instruction, or government of any kind; only, if one was riotous, he had her brought upon deck, and put into a thing like a watch-box, in which they could not sit, and could only just stand upright. It was very strongly built: no opening, except some small holes at the top to admit air. The women were sometimes shut up in this for hours at a time."[90]

Prisoners who survived the journey were housed in factories, where they were made to work until they received more specific assignments such as becoming farmhands or servants for the wealthy colonial settlers. In the factories, they were managed by matrons who had overall charge of rations, which were often so paltry that, in the Parramatta Female Factory, at least one inmate died of starvation.

Reformers were concerned about the extent of immorality among the prisoners, and recommended that:

"Married woman convicted of felonies should either not be transported at all, or they should be divorced, or have the same privilege granted to them as the men, provided their husbands are willing to follow them. Women in a penal settlement, fettered with distant ties, are in a position in which vice is inevitable; and nothing can justify deliberately placing them in it. During their first two stages, women should not, I think, ever be seen out of their penitentiary, nor should any male be admitted into it, or have direct authority over it, except the principal superintendent of the settlement, the chaplain, and surgeon."[91]

More positively, only a relatively small proportion of prisoners were transported for life, and those who completed their sentences were free to return to Britain. Many, though, could not afford the passage home; while others believed that they could create a better life for themselves in the colonies.

"They did not generally seem to be dejected, nor to regard transportation as a punishment," boatswain Owens reported, "A great many said they never meant to go back to England."[92]

There were several reasons why a death sentence might be commuted to transportation, one of which was that the condemned prisoner was pregnant. Such was the case of Mary Ann Hunt who, in 1847, beat her elderly landlady, Mrs Stowell, to death with a poker so that she could rob her. She was arrested almost immediately and, despite evidence that she was prone to fits and had no recollection of the murder, she was found guilty. When the Clerk of the Court asked the euphemistic question about whether there were any reason why she should not be sentenced to death, she replied that she was pregnant.

The jury of matrons who examined her took far longer than usual to decide that she was mistaken, and so the judge pronounced the death sentence. In the execution cell in Newgate, she continued to insist that she was pregnant, and, when a medical officer examined her, he came to the same conclusion. The story caused a sensation as the public waited eagerly to discover who was correct; and lawyers and doctors wrote to the press, complaining about the practice of employing untrained matrons to make a diagnosis.

In view of the conflicting reports, the judge reported the case to the Home Secretary, George Grey, and ordered

Mary Ann to remain in prison pending his reply. Having read the reports, Grey wrote to the aldermen of Newgate:

"With reference to the case of Mary Ann Hunt, the convict under sentence of death in the gaol of Newgate, in which case the Sheriffs, for reasons reported to me, directed that the execution of the sentence should be delayed, and afterwards, by command of her Majesty, the capital sentence was respited until further order should be given, I have the honour to inform you, that, under the special circumstances which have occurred in this case, her Majesty has been pleased to command that that sentence should not be carried into effect. I request that you will communicate to the prisoner this information. The prisoner will be detained in Newgate until after her expected confinement, when the commuted punishment will be notified."[93]

Only a month later, Mary Ann gave birth to a healthy baby boy, which begs the question: how could the matrons have failed to notice that she was eight months pregnant?

When she had recovered, Grey commuted her sentence to transportation, ordering her first to spend two years in prison in England, raising her child until he was old enough to accompany her to the colonies.

Mary Ann thrived in Tasmania, where she eventually married a fellow convict and, twenty-five years after murdering Mrs Stowell, she was granted a free pardon.

A year after the murder of Mrs Sowell, Private Henry Ducker of the Coldstream Guards was walking out of Wellington Barracks into Birdcage Walk when a young woman approached him from behind and shot him dead with a single bullet to the back of the head. Twenty-five-year-old Annette Myers then threw down the pistol and calmly walked on in the direction of Buckingham Palace until a policeman, who had witnessed the episode, apprehended her.

"I did it;" she said frankly. "I intended to do it; I have intended to do it for a long time."

At the station, she co-operated fully with the investigation, explaining that she had arrived in England from France eight years earlier to work as a housemaid for her uncle, a distinguished lawyer, Sir Francis Myers[dd]. Since then, she had been in service with various employers, and had made the acquaintance of Private Ducker, with whom she had an affair.

Ducker had treated her appallingly. He regularly asked her for money and, when she had none left to give, he told her to pawn her clothes and to take up prostitution and, when she refused, he abandoned her. Moreover, Annette told the police, he was simultaneously involved with several other women, from whom he also extracted money; and, as evidence, she handed over a collection of explicit and desperate letters, which she had sent to her lover. When her rooms were searched, the police found further correspondence, demonstrating the extent to which Ducker had mistreated her.

Although Annette was clearly guilty of murder, the press and public were united in viewing Ducker as the guilty party.

> "The fate," wrote the prison reformer, Thomas Beggs, "to which in a moment of desperation she doomed the man who had excited, and then trampled upon, an ardent and misplaced affection is merciful to that to which she would have fallen had she yielded to his suggestions. He had won her love, and tried to use the ascendancy it gave him over her, to the most wicked of all purposes. He wanted

---

[dd] It is highly likely that Annette was in fact Sir Francis' illegitimate daughter.

means to sustain his debaucheries, and was willing to procure them by the poor girl's prostitution. Many such men there are who meet with no earthly avenger, systematically debauching youth and living on the price of blood!"[94]

When the sordid details of her affair were made public during her trial at the Old Bailey, she became increasingly agitated, further exciting public sympathy. Nonetheless, in view of her confession, the jury was obliged to find her guilty but they strongly recommended mercy on the grounds of extreme provocation. The judge, Mr Justice Coltman was far less compassionate as he opined that the cold-blooded killing was premeditated and, unless such crimes were severely punished, the whole of society would be in danger. Even so, when he donned the black cap and uttered the death sentence, he was seen to weep, as did the crowds both in and outside the courtroom.

Message of support for Annette poured in from across the country; and the satirical magazine *Punch*, comparing her crime to that of a duellist defending his honour, urged Queen Victoria to show clemency:

"Yet she may hold her blood-stain'd hand
Up with the noblest of the land.
Ye who from slander's slightest breath
Would purge your precious fame,
Who would avenge unto the death
An insult to your name.
What would you do – have done, in fact –
Less than the frantic woman's act?
Victoria, in thy courtly train
The duellist goes free.
One hast thou pardon'd in thy reign,
Spite of the law's decree;
Pity and precedent may strive
To save this erring soul alive."[95]

Even Ducker's family wrote to their M.P., William Ewart, urging him to do all in his power to obtain a reprieve. When the case was later discussed in the House of Commons, Ewart commented that 'it speaks well for that family, that they had such a feeling; but it was a feeling that was participated in almost through the whole country.'[96]

Ultimately, the Home Secretary commuted the sentence to two years in the Westminster Bridewell in Tothill Fields[ee], followed by transportation for life.

During the first few months of her imprisonment, Annette sank into such a deep depression that there was some question as to whether she were sane enough to complete her sentence, but, by October 1850, she was sufficiently recovered to join one-hundred-and-sixty-nine other female convicts aboard the *Emma Eugenia* bound for Van Diemen's Land[ff].

Annette created a reasonable life for herself in Tasmania, working as a servant and marrying a fellow convict before obtaining a conditional pardon in 1856. She died in Australia in 1879, having spent over twenty-nine years in the colonies.

One of Annette's fellow-prisoners on the *Emma Eugenia* was thirty-one-year-old Ann Merritt, whose controversial case divided public opinion.

In January 1850, she had been married to James Merritt for seven years and had borne him five children, two of whom died in infancy. Although not rich, they lived comfortably in Pear Tree Place in Clapton, where James worked as a turncock with the East London Waterworks Company. On 24th January, he vomited before leaving for work but he settled his stomach with a tot of rum in a pub on the way to the waterworks company.

---

[ee] The now demolished prison stood on the site now occupied by Westminster Cathedral.

[ff] Transportation to New South Wales had been abolished in 1850.

At lunchtime, he felt a little better but had not regained his appetite and he refused the meal that Ann had prepared for him. Instead, she gave him a bowl of gruel, which he half-heartedly ate before returning to work but, by mid-afternoon, he felt so ill that he was sent home. He took to his bed, complaining of a burning pain in his chest, stomach and limbs; and, in the evening, he deteriorated so rapidly that Ann sought help from her neighbour Mary Gillett.

Mrs Gillett's first thought was that James had brought the sickness on himself as he had recently taken to drinking, but, seeing him, she was so alarmed that she ran to fetch a doctor. At about half-past ten, Dr Toulmin arrived and, having examined the patient, made up a prescription of calomel and opium. The following morning, Dr Toulmin received word that James was dead.

The doctor's initial response was to recommend a post-mortem but Ann, sobbing and distraught, gasped that James would not want such a procedure. As Toulmin had always known her to be a good wife and mother, he accepted her decision and let the matter drop.

The coroner was far less accommodating, and found the case so perturbing that he insisted on a thorough investigation. James' innards were sent for analysis to Dr Henry Letheby, Professor of Chemistry at the London Hospital, who detected a quantity of arsenic in the stomach and small intestine. He concluded that the poison had been administered two to three hours prior to death.

> "The time would not depend on the constitution of the person. Digestion depends upon the constitution, but I am speaking of the average. Digestion is more or less rapid according to the constitution of the person who has received the subject matter."[97]

Inspector Coward arrested Ann Merritt, who wept that she loved her husband far too much to ever wrong or injure 'the poor dear soul'; and she denied ever purchasing arsenic. In the course of Coward's investigations, a chemist stated that he had sold arsenic to Mrs Merritt and, when this was put to her, she altered her story. She had bought it, she said, intending to kill herself because she and James were so unhappy together; and, after further reflection, she suggested that James might have mistaken it for baking soda; or perhaps he had taken it on purpose because he had some financial difficulties.

During her trial, several witnesses including Dr Toulmin attested to her good character, but Dr Letheby's testimony was pivotal to the prosecution's case. If the poison were ingested two or three hours prior to death, Ann was the only person who could have administered it. The jury found her guilty with a recommendation to mercy on account of her good character, but the judge appeared unmoved as he passed the death sentence.

Fortunately for Ann, several medical men had attended the trial and they were so astonished by Dr Letheby's evidence that they wrote to the Home Secretary, explaining that it was impossible to fix the time when the poison had been administered. This attack on his professional judgement was so offensive to Dr Letheby that he, too, wrote to the Home Secretary, admitting that he had been mistaken about the timing; and, in view of this error, Ann's sentence was commuted to transportation.

As a result of his mistake, Letheby's reputation was permanently damaged, and he suffered furthered humiliation when the Liberal M.P. John Bright cited him as an example of the dangers of capital punishment.

"On what ground was she sentenced?" Bright asked. "On the opinion of a medical man, who appears to have given a rash of unscientific opinion, and which was afterwards strongly contradicted by the opinions of others of the same profession."

In an effort to redeem himself, Letheby claimed credit for having Ann's sentence commuted.

"I was the cause of her being respited and the sentence was not carried into effect, in consequence of a letter I wrote to the Home Office. Other scientific gentlemen interfered, and challenged the soundness of my conclusions before I wrote that letter. I have not since been employed by the Crown."[98]

Ann, meanwhile, set sail for Van Diemen's Land on the *Emma Eugenia,* leaving her children to the care of the workhouse. Unlike Annette Myers, she had little time to forge a new life in the colonies, for she died two years later at the age of only thirty-four.

Her death coincided with an alteration to the law on transportation. The 1853 Penal Servitude Act abolished the punishment for anyone who was not serving a life sentence; and ended all transportation to Tasmania. Four years later, a further Penal Servitude Act paved the way for the complete abolition of the practice, reducing the number of convict ships to one per year until 1867, when the *Hougoumont* took the last group of prisoners to the colonies.

# Chapter 20 - And Finally...A Mystery

Five years after the trial of Madeleine Smith[gg], the case was still fresh in the minds of Glaswegians when an even more controversial murder took place within a mile of the Smith family home.

A highly-respected widowed accountant, John Fleming, lived at 17 Sandyford Place, Glasgow, with his eighty-seven-year-old father, James; his son; two daughters; his sister and a number of servants. Being a man of considerable means, John Fleming also owned a house in the country to which most of the household repaired every summer. Work commitments kept him and his son in the city from Monday to Friday, but at weekends they, too, escaped to the country, leaving John's elderly father and one trusted servant, Jessie McPherson, as the sole occupants of the property in Glasgow.

On Monday, 7th July 1862, John and his son returned to the city as usual and went straight to their office before going home to Sandyford Place in the late afternoon. Normally, the servant opened the door to admit them, so they were surprised when, this afternoon, it was opened by John's father. When asked where Jessie was, the old man replied that he had not seen her since Friday as she had 'cut' – meaning she had left without giving any explanation or notice – and that her room in the basement was locked.

John's first thought might have been that his father had driven the girl away, for, in spite of his age, James Fleming had a reputation for seducing female servants. John's son, however, was more concerned for Jessie's safety, fearing that she might be ill or even have died within her locked room. All three men went down to the basement, where John located a spare key, and, on

---

[gg] See Chapter 5

unlocking the room, he found Jessie lying dead on the floor, half-naked and covered in blood.

Presuming that she had killed herself, he sent for a physician, Dr Watson, who, having counted more than forty injuries to the body, stated categorically that she had been murdered.

The police searched the house and found bloodstains in the kitchen sink, and trail of blood through the hallway as though the body had been dragged into the bedroom. It was clear that some attempt had been made to scrub the paving stones in the kitchen and, more surprisingly, part of Jessie's face had also been washed. When splatters of blood were also found on two of James Fleming's shirts, he became the prime suspect.

The Sheriff of Lanarkshire, Sir Archibald Alison, questioned him for over four hours and found that 'his conduct after the murder had been extremely suspicious.'[99] He said that he had heard screams in the early hours of Saturday morning but, presuming they came from the drunks who often gathered in the adjacent ally, he had ignored them. He admitted, too, that he had noticed the blood splatters on his shirts but had no idea where they came from; and he had not been in the least concerned about the servant's unexplained absence.

Although there was no sign of a break-in, a quantity of silver plate was missing, as were some of Jessie's possessions and clothes. When a list of the stolen items was printed in the press, a pawnbroker reported that a married woman, Jessie M'Lachlan, had brought the silver to his shop. The police learned that Jessie M'Lachlan was not only the Flemings' former maid, but also a friend of the victim, Jessie McPherson.

During a brief search of the M'Lachlans' home, the police found the victim's clothes, and bloodstains on Jessie M'Lachlan's dress. She and her husband, James, were arrested but, when the latter proved he had been away at sea at the time of the murder, he was released without charge.

Mrs M'Lachlan denied having been near Sandyford Place on the fatal weekend, and, when asked how she came by the stolen silver, she gave the unlikely explanation that old Mr Fleming had brought it to her to ask her to pawn it for him as he was short of money while his son way away in the country. She was, though, unable to explain why she had the dead woman's clothes; and, when a cast was made of her foot, it was found to match a bloody footprint from the scene of the murder.

From the moment that Jessie M'Lachlan was charged with murder, large sections of the press and public questioned the evidence against her. As she and the victim had been friends for over four years, was it likely that, for the sake of some second-hand clothes and few pieces of silver, a young mother would commit such a violent murder?

> "It is very strange," the Glasgow Herald reported, "if plunder was the object the murderer had in view, that a sum of money which lay on a shelf in McPherson's bedroom was left untouched, and also that several articles of silver plate, including a cruet-stand, were left beside the body."[100]

Many journalists asked why the police had been so quick to arrest her, while ignoring equally strong evidence against James Fleming. Her advocate, Mr Clark, seized on this point during her trial, when he subjected the old man to a lengthy cross-examination. Mr Fleming retained his composure but contradicted himself several times regarding his behaviour on the Saturday morning. He initially claimed he had stayed in bed until nine o'clock, but also admitted that he opened the door to the milkman who called at the house somewhere between eight and nine. It was surely the servant's job to answer the door, said Mr Clark, so why had James Fleming done so unless he knew that the maid was dead? Fleming replied tellingly that she *was* dead by the Saturday morning, but he added that he was unaware of that at the time. In response to further questions, he said he had made his own meals throughout the weekend, yet he had not noticed the blood in the kitchen sink or on the floor; nor had he questioned why, if the servant had simply 'cut', she had bothered to lock her bedroom door.

Mr Clark then turned to Mr Fleming's character, particularly regarding his behaviour towards female servants. It was alleged that he had previously made one girl pregnant; and a friend of Jessie McPherson attested that she had met her shortly before the murder and, seeing how pale and ill she looked, she had asked her what was the matter. Jessie McPherson had replied that she was very unhappy about being left alone with James Fleming who was 'actually an old wretch and an old devil.'

This evidence was quickly dismissed by the judge, Lord Deas, who told the jury to disregard this statement, as it was merely an opinion with no basis in fact. Mr Clark's attempts to lay the blame on Fleming were further weakened by the testimony of the medical examiner, Dr George MacLeod, who, from the start, was convinced of the old man's innocence. Describing Fleming's behaviour when he was asked to identify the body, he said:

> "...His manner...was such when performing this duty – which is often so trying to those unaccustomed to the sight of dead bodies – and afterwards, when on different occasions [I] had to examine his person, as impressed [me] strongly with a conviction of the non-participation of this individual in the crime."[101]

Even more damaging to Mrs M'Lachlan's defence was MacLeod's insistence that the murderer must have been a woman, as demonstrated by the wounds that the victim sustained during a frenzied attack:

"If a strong man," he said, "had been influenced by such passion, and had been armed with such a weapon as there was reason to believe had been used here, the skull would have been driven in at many places (and it was rather a thin skull), and not merely at one point where many blows had been concentrated. The shallow notches all over the side of the skull did not evidence either the strength or the even-down blows of a man."[102]

What was more, ten days after the murder, MacLeod discovered teeth marks on Mrs M'Lachlan's hand; and, although she claimed to have been bitten by a dog, three surgeons concurred that the marks were human, and were probably caused by Jessie McPherson, fighting for her life. When, on the other hand, MacLeod examined James Fleming, he observed that: 'on no part of his body was there a scratch to be found indicative of a personal encounter, or a drop of blood on any of his clothes, all of which had the appearances of having been worn for several days.'[103]

Mrs McLachlan's supporters could be forgiven for thinking that the authorities were doing their utmost to protect James Fleming at the defendant's expense. On the final day of the hearing, Lord Deas entered the court carrying his black cap as though he were telling the jury that he expected a guilty verdict; and, in the four hours he spent summing up the case, he discounted Fleming as a suspect, while placing great emphasis on the evidence against Jessie M'Lachlan. The effect was so powerful that the jury took only fifteen minutes to return a guilty verdict.

Although prisoners were not permitted to give evidence during their trial, they were allowed to make a statement once the verdict had been returned. Lord Deas, therefore, asked if Mrs M'Lachlan had anything to say, to which Mr Clark replied that he would read a statement that she had prepared in advance. In fact, she had made the statement before the trial began, but her advocate had decided not to use it because it placed her at the scene of the crime when she had initially denied being in the area. Now, though, with nothing to lose, he was about to enliven the proceedings with her explosive account of what actually happened on the night of the murder.

She claimed that she regularly visited Jessie McPherson on Friday evenings after James Fleming had gone to bed, when the rest of the household was away in the country. On Friday 4th July, she had taken a bottle of rum to share with her friend but was surprised to find the old man was still up, sitting in the kitchen. All three shared the rum and some whisky, which Fleming provided, and when the bottles were empty, he asked Mrs M'Lachlan to go out and buy some more.

She set out for the shop but, as it was closed, she returned empty-handed to Sandyford Place. Fleming opened the back door to let her in, and she followed him into the kitchen, asking where Jessie was, as it was now nearly midnight and she wished to say good night before leaving. When he did not reply, she followed him into the hallway, where she heard a low moaning coming from Jessie's room. She pushed open the door and found her friend lying half-dressed and semi-conscious in a pool of blood.

"Why have you done this!" she cried to Fleming, sending him to fetch some warm water, as she crouched to tend Jessie's wounds. As she began to revive, Mrs M'Lachlan offered to bring a doctor but the injured woman begged her not to leave her alone with Fleming.

With the old man's help, Mrs M'Lachlan lifted her friend onto the bed and bathed her cuts while Fleming wandered in and out, cleaning up the blood.

As she regained more strength, Jessie McPherson explained that, a couple of weeks earlier, James Fleming had climbed into her bed and attempted to rape her. When she threatened to tell his son, he offered her money to buy her silence but, since then, there had been a lot of tension between them. This evening, she said, when Mrs M'Lachlan had gone out to buy more whisky, she had gone to her room to prepare for bed. The old man had followed her and, when she slammed the door to keep him out, he forced his way in and hit her in the face with a heavy object.

Fleming, hearing what she was saying, did not deny it, but, when she added that now she would have to report him, he offered her more money to remain quiet, and told Mrs M'Lachlan to swear on the Bible that she would never speak about what had happened.

For the next few hours, the two women lay on the bed together but, at three o'clock in the morning, Jessie McPherson awoke complaining that she was cold. Fleming and Mrs M'Lachlan helped her into the kitchen so she could lie beside the fire but, after a couple of hours, she felt so unwell that she asked for a doctor.

Jessie M'Lachlan intended to bring a surgeon but, when she tried to leave the house, she found the backdoor locked and the key was missing. She tried the other doors, and, when it became clear that Fleming had locked them all to prevent her from leaving, she decided to climb out of the window. She was about to do so when she heard such pitiful cries that she hurried back to the kitchen in time to see Fleming beating Jessie to death with a cleaver.

She screamed and fled, certain that he intended to murder her, too, but he called after her urgently, promising not to harm her. It was obvious, he said, that Jessie McPherson was dying and no one could have saved her, but if a doctor had come to the house, she would have told him what had happened. Now, he warned, if Mrs M'Lachlan told the police that he had killed her, he would deny it and say that *she* was the murderer. Whom were the police more likely to believe: an elderly man from a respectable family, or a former servant who was constantly short of money? If, on the other hand, she would help him make it appear that her friend had been killed during a robbery, he would see to it that she was amply rewarded.

Terrified into believing that she had no other option, Mrs M'Lachlan helped him to move the body and clean up some of the blood. He then told her take the dead woman's clothes and the silver plate; and at eight o'clock in the morning, he unlocked the door and let her leave.

For forty minutes, the court sat in stunned silence as Mr Clark read out the statement, and, when he had finished, many expected Lord Deas to order a retrial. True to form, however, he reiterated that James Fleming had nothing to do with the murder, and that Mrs M'Lachlan's statement was:

> "...a tissue of as wicked falsehoods as any to which I ever listened, and in place of tending to rest any suspicion against the man whom you wished to implicate, I think if anything were wanting to satisfy the public mind of that man's innocence it would be that most incredible statement, which you have now made."[104]

In conclusion, he praised the jury's intelligence in coming to the correct verdict, before donning the black cap and sentencing Jessie M'Lachlan to death.

The statement, however, had caused such a sensation across the country that, from meetings, discussions and protest groups, support for Mrs M'Lachlan escalated. It was widely believed that the evidence against James Fleming was at least as strong as that against the convicted woman, and that he had been discounted as a suspect solely because of his family's connections. Prominent citizens were likewise concerned about a miscarriage of justice, as the Sheriff, Sir Archibald Alison, wrote:

"A calm consideration of the case would have led to a verdict of the theft proven, but the murder not proven."[105]

Some argued that it would have been impossible for Mrs M'Lachlan to have acted alone, as she would not have had the strength to inflict so many wounds on her friend before dragging a lifeless body from the kitchen to the bedroom. Others suggested that it was highly unlikely that she would have murdered Jessie McPherson solely to steal some second-hand clothes and a few pieces of silver, when the house was filled with more valuable items.

Naturally, petitions were sent to the Home Secretary, George Grey, who not only sought the opinion of a number of legal and medical advisors, but also asked George Young, the Sheriff of Haddington, to undertake an inquiry into the trial and Mrs M'Lachlan's final statement. To allow Young time to complete his work, Grey ordered a stay of execution but warned the prisoner not to hope that this would lead to a reprieve.

Young began by confirming that Mrs M'Lachlan had made her statement before the trial began, which led him to conclude that her defence counsel ought to have presented it sooner. As it was, it had unjustly imputed Fleming when he was not in a position to deny the accusations; and it would have been better if Lord Deas had prevented Clark from reading it. Under Scottish law, a trial witness could not afterwards stand trial on a charge related to the original crime, and, therefore, although Fleming's reputation had been sullied, there was no means by which he could clear his name.

Nonetheless, Young also noted that Jessie M'Lachlan's version of events was supported by the evidence of disinterested witnesses. One woman, for example, who happened to be passing, heard the low moans that Jessie had described, whereas Fleming had claimed that he had heard screaming. Young drew attention, too, to the evidence of a woman who scrubbed the steps of the house, and who attested that Mr Fleming had asked her to clean up a bloody footprint, which appeared to have been covered in soot. Finally, he pointed out that there was 'a good deal' of evidence to suggest that the old man had indeed behaved improperly towards female servants. At the age of seventy-seven, he had fathered an illegitimate child; and he had paid unwelcome attention to Jessie McPherson. Jessie M'Lachlan had claimed that the deceased said Fleming had attempted to rape her on a specific Friday night after he had returned from drinking with a friend. Young found sufficient circumstantial evidence to support the veracity of this statement.

Ultimately, though, Young concluded that, even if Fleming's guilt were proved, it would not exculpate Mrs M'Lachlan. From her own confession, it was clear that she had been at least an accessory, and had profited to the tune of seven pounds from stealing from her friend and concealing the truth about her murder.

On 24<sup>th</sup> October, Young sent the findings of his secret inquiry to the Home Secretary, who commuted Jessie M'Lachlan's sentence to life imprisonment. Although her life had been spared, this outcome satisfied no one, for, as several politicians argued, if she were guilty of murder she ought to be hanged; and if she were innocent, she should be released. Petitions were sent to the Prime Minister, Palmerston, asking him to intervene and publicise the reasons why the sentence had been commuted; and when the case was debated in the House of Commons, there were calls for the establishment of Court of Appeal in Scotland, so that prisoners, like Mrs M'Lachlan, could receive a fairer hearing.

The Flemings were so disturbed by this turn of events that they wrote to the Home Secretary, asking him to issue a statement that 'the alteration upon the sentence was not intended to lead to the inference that, in his judgment,

Mr Fleming was otherwise than innocent of the murder.'
Grey refused their request, and when they pressed him
again, his representative replied that:

> "…The result of the inquiry was far from removing
> all uncertainty, nor could it be justly held to fix a
> share of the guilt on any other person, especially
> when such person was not represented at the
> inquiry. With reference to your present request, it is
> not in Sir George Grey's power to direct a judicial
> inquiry to be held upon the guilt or innocence of
> any person not charged with any offence, especially
> when, as in the present case, according to what he is
> informed is the law of Scotland, the person on
> whose behalf you make the request having been
> examined as a witness in a criminal trial, cannot
> afterwards be subjected to a criminal prosecution in
> respect of the matter of such trial."[106]

Consequently, it would be impossible for James
Fleming to clear his name, or to face charges for his alleged
involvement in the murder.

Jessie M'Lachlan was transferred to Perth Prison to
begin her life sentence, while the repercussions of the case
rippled through her family. The notoriety was so great that
her husband emigrated with their young son to the United
States; and her sister was dismissed from service solely
because of her relationship to a convicted murderer.

Jessie's defence team continued to argue for a
reprieve but it was not until 1877, fifteen years into her
sentence, that she was finally released on licence. She, too,
emigrated to America where she eventually remarried and
died in Michigan in 1899.

Did Jessie M'Lachlan kill Jessie McPherson? Had
she conspired with James Fleming to murder her friend? Or
was she another of Fleming's victims, whom he had
terrified into concealing the truth that *he* had murdered
Jessie?

# Index of Murderesses & Alleged Murderesses

# By the Same Author:

## Biography & History

*Queen Victoria's Granddaughters 1960-1918*
*Queen Victoria's Grandsons 1859-1918*
*Queen Victoria's Cousins*
*Queen Victoria's Creatures – Royalty & Animals in the Victoria Era*
*Alice, the Enigma – A Biography of Queen Victoria's Daughter*
*Dear Papa, Beloved Mama – An intimate portrait of Queen Victoria & Prince Albert as parents*
*The Innocence of Kaiser Wilhelm II*
*Queen Victoria & The French Royal Families*
*Thunder of Freedom – The British Suffragette Movement*
*Queen Victoria & Her Prime Ministers*

## Historical Fiction

*Most Beautiful Princess – A Novel Based on the Life of Grand Duchess Elizabeth of Russia*
*Shattered Crowns: The Scapegoats*
*Shattered Crowns: The Sacrifice*
*Shattered Crowns: The Betrayal*
*The Fields Laid Waste*

## Novels

*The Counting House*
*By Any Other Name*
*The Goose Girl*

## Poetry & Children's Books

*Wonderful Walter*
*Child of the Moon*
*The Ragamuffin Sun*

# References

1 Anon. *The Groans of the Gallows* (1855)
2 Hansard HC Deb 10 March 1853 vol 124 cc1414-22
3 Wynn Westcott, W. *Twelve Years' Experience as a London Coroner* (Ballière, Tindall & Cox 1907)
4 Swaine Taylor, Alfred *Medical Jurisprudence* (John Churchill 1861)
5 Mayhew, Henry *The Criminal Prisons Of London* (Griffin, Bohn & Company 1862)
6 Hansard (HL Deb 15 June 1866 vol 184 cc451-64)
7 Hansard (HL Deb 15 June 1866 vol 184 cc451-64)
8 Berry, James *My Experiences As An Executioner* (Percy Lund & Co. 1905)
9 London Medical Gazette Vol 38 (1846)
10 Buxton, Sydney *A Handbook to the Political Questions of the Day* (John Murray 1882)
11 Usher, J.E. *Alcoholism & its Treatment* (Baillière, Tindall & Cox 1892)
12 Bronte, Anne *The Tenant of Wildfell Hall* (1848)
13 Dickens, Charles *Sketches by Boz* (1837)
14 Sherlock, Frederick *Ann Jane Carlile; a Temperance Pioneer* (1897)
15 Sherlock, Frederick *Ann Jane Carlile; a Temperance Pioneer* (1897)
16 Swaine Taylor, Alfred *Medical Jurisprudence* (John Churchill 1861)
17 Dickens, Charles, *Household Words Vol XII* (Bradbury & Evans 1856)
18 Swaine Taylor, Alfred *Medical Jurisprudence* (John Churchill 1861)
19 Roughead, William *Twelve Scots Trials* (W. Green & Sons 1913)
20 Roughead, William *Twelve Scots Trials* (W. Green & Sons 1913)
21 Hansard HL Deb 23 April 1847 vol 91 cc1240-1
22 Berry, James *My Experiences As An Executioner* (Percy Lund & Co. 1905)
23 MacDougall, Alexander *The Maybrick Case* (Baillière, Tindall & Cox 1891)
24 MacDougall, Alexander *The Maybrick Case* (Baillière, Tindall & Cox 1891)
25 Maybrick, Florence *My Fifteen Lost Years* (Funk & Wagnall's Co. 1905)
26 Irving, H.B. *The Trial of Mrs Maybrick* (William Hodge & Co. 1912)
27 Roughead, William *Glengarry's Way* (W. Green & Son 1932)
28 London Medical Gazette Vol 38 (1846)
29 Roughead, William *Twelve Scots Trials* (W. Green & Sons 1913)
30 Duncan Smith, A. *The Trial of Madeleine Smith* (William Hodge & Company 1905)
31 Duncan Smith, A. *The Trial of Madeleine Smith* (William Hodge & Company 1905)
32 Duncan Smith, A. *The Trial of Madeleine Smith* (William Hodge & Company 1905)
33 Disraeli, Benjamin *Sybil* (1845)
34 Hall, Sir John *The Trial of Adelaide Bartlett* (Butterworth & Co. 1927)
35 Walker-Smith, Derek *The Life of Sir Edward Clarke* (Thornton Butterworth 1939)
36 Hall, Sir John *The Trial of Adelaide Bartlett* (Butterworth & Co. 1927)
37 Clarke, Sir Edward *The Story of my Life* (E.F. Dutton & Co. 1919)
38 Hall, Sir John *The Trial of Adelaide Bartlett* (Butterworth & Co. 1927)
39 Hall, Sir John *The Trial of Adelaide Bartlett* (Butterworth & Co. 1927)
40 Yellowlees, David *Lunacy & Pauperism* (Glasgow Poor Law Conference 1884)
41 Forbes Winslow *The Journal of Psychological Medicine and Mental Pathology Vol. VII* (John Churchill 1854)
42 Forbes Winslow *The Journal of Psychological Medicine and Mental Pathology Vol. VII* (John Churchill 1854)
43 Robinson, F.W. *Female Life in Prison* (Rose Publishing 1888)
44 Robinson, F.W. *Female Life in Prison* (Rose Publishing 1888)
45 Forbes Winslow, L. *Recollections of Forty Years* (John Ouseley Ltd. 1910)
46 Forbes Winslow, L. *Recollections of Forty Years* (John Ouseley Ltd. 1910)
47 Hawkins, Henry, Baron Brampton *The Reminiscences of Sir Henry Hawkins, Baron Brampton* (Edward Arnold 1904)

[48] Burke Ryan, William *Infanticide: Its Law, Prevalence, Prevention & History* (Churchill 1862)

[49] More Madden, Thomas *Puerperal Mania* (J.E. Adlard 1871)

[50] More Madden, Thomas *Puerperal Mania* (J.E. Adlard 1871)

[51] Philips, F.C. *My Varied Life* (E.Nash 1914)

[52] Robinson, F.W. *Female Life in Prison* (Rose Publishing 1888)

[53] Pankhurst, Emmeline *My Own Story* (Eveleigh Nash 1914)

[54] Forbes Winslow, L. *The Insanity of Passion & Crime* (John Ouseley Ltd. 1912)

[55] Lytton, Lady Constance *Prisons & Prisoners* (William Heinemann 1914)

[56] Robinson, F.W. *Female Life in Prison* (Rose Publishing 1888)

[57] Robinson, F.W. *Female Life in Prison* (Rose Publishing 1888)

[58] Creighton, M. *A Memoir of Sir George Grey* (Longmans, Green & Co. 1901)

[59] Robinson, F.W. *Female Life in Prison* (Rose Publishing 1888)

[60] Robinson, F.W. *Female Life in Prison* (Rose Publishing 1888)

[61] Fairfield, George *Some Account of George William Wilshere, Baron Bramwell* (Macmillan & Co. 1898)

[62] Greenwood, James *The Seven Curses of London* (1869)

[63] Pankhurst, Emmeline *My Own Story* (Eveleigh Nash 1914)

[64] Forbes Winslow, L. *Recollections of Forty Years* (John Ouseley Ltd. 1910)

[65] Forbes Winslow, L. *Recollections of Forty Years* (John Ouseley Ltd. 1910))

[66] Forbes Winslow, L. *Recollections of Forty Years* (John Ouseley Ltd. 1910)

[67] Waugh, Benjamin *Baby-Farming* (Kegan, Paul, Trench, Trubner & Co. 1890)

[68] Roughead, William *Glengarry's Way* (W. Green & Son 1932)

[69] Hansard HC Deb 10 June 1856 vol 142 cc1231-61

[70] Montagu Williams, Stephen *Leaves of a Life* (Macmillan 1893)

[71] Montagu Williams, Stephen *Leaves of a Life* (Macmillan 1893)

[72] Follen Folsom, Charles *Studies in Criminal Responsibility* (1909)

[73] British Medical Journal Vol 1 (1871)

[74] British Medical Journal Vol 1 (1871)

[75] Follen Folsom, Charles *Studies in Criminal Responsibility* (1909)

[76] Berry, James *My Experiences As An Executioner* (Percy Lund & Co. 1905)

[77] Berry, James *My Experiences As An Executioner* (Percy Lund & Co. 1905)

[78] Beeton, Isabella *Household Management* (S.O. Beeton 1861)

[79] Beeton, Isabella *Household Management* (S.O. Beeton 1861)

[80] Austin, E. *Anecdotage* (F. Pitman 1872)

[81] Anon. *The Bermondsey Murder: A Full Report of the Trial of Frederick George Manning & Maria Manning* (W.M. Clarke 1849)

[82] Wyndham, Horace *Feminine Frailty* (Ernest Benn Ltd. 1929)

[83] Anon. *The Bermondsey Murder: A Full Report of the Trial of Frederick George Manning & Maria Manning* (W.M. Clarke 1849)

[84] Wyndham, Horace *Feminine Frailty* (Ernest Benn Ltd. 1929)

[85] Ballantine, William *Some Experiences of A Barrister's Life* (Henry Holt & Co. 1882)

[86] Dickens, Charles *Letter to the Times 13th November 1849* (The British Library)

[87] Robinson, F.W. *Female Life in Prison* (Rose Publishing 1888)

[88] Robinson, F.W. *Female Life in Prison* (Rose Publishing 1888)

[89] Robinson, F.W. *Female Life in Prison* (Rose Publishing 1888)

[90] Whately, Richard, Archbishop of Dublin *Remarks on Transportation – A Letter to Earl Grey* (B. Fellowes 1834)

[91] MacOnochie, Alexander *Benevolence in Punishment* (Seeley, Burnside & Seeley 1845)

[92] Whately, Richard, Archbishop of Dublin *Remarks on Transportation – A Letter to Earl Grey* (B. Fellowes 1834)

[93] *London Medical Gazette Vol 5* (1847)

[94] Beggs, Thomas *Juvenile Depravity* (Charles Gilpin 1849)

[95] Punch Magazine (March 1848)
[96] Hansard *HC Deb 01 May 1849 vol 104 cc1058-90*
[97] Lathom Browne, G & Stewart, C.G. *Reports of Trials for Murder by Poisoning* (Stevens & Sons 1883)
[98] Lathom Browne, G & Stewart, C.G. *Reports of Trials for Murder by Poisoning* (Stevens & Sons 1883)
[99] Alison, Sir Archibald *Some Account of my Life & Writing* (W. Blackwood 1883)
[100] Roughead, William *Trial of Mrs M'Lachlan* (William Hodge & Co. 1911)
[101] MacLeod, George *An Account of the Medical Evidence Connected with the Trial of Jessie M'Lachlan, at the Glasgow Autumn Circuit, 1862* (William Mackenzie 1862)
[102] MacLeod, George *An Account of the Medical Evidence Connected with the Trial of Jessie M'Lachlan, at the Glasgow Autumn Circuit, 1862* (William Mackenzie 1862)
[103] MacLeod, George *An Account of the Medical Evidence Connected with the Trial of Jessie M'Lachlan, at the Glasgow Autumn Circuit, 1862* (William Mackenzie 1862)
[104] Roughead, William *Trial of Mrs M'Lachlan* (William Hodge & Co. 1911)
[105] Alison, Sir Archibald *Some Account of my Life & Writing* (W. Blackwood 1883)
[106] Roughead, William *Trial of Mrs M'Lachlan* (William Hodge & Co. 1911)

Printed in Dunstable, United Kingdom